HALFWAY HOUSE
TO HEAVEN

HALFWAY HOUSE TO HEAVEN

Unravelling the mystery of the majestic River Oxus

BILL COLEGRAVE

BENE FACTUM PUBLISHING

For Soraya, as beautiful as the Wakhan, and for three fellow travellers
sans pareil Benjiamino, Siena and Kara Paloma

Halfway House to Heaven
Unravelling the mystery of the majestic River Oxus

First published in 2010 by
Bene Factum Publishing Ltd
PO Box 58122
London
SW8 5WZ

Email: inquiries@bene-factum.co.uk
www.bene-factum.co.uk

ISBN: 978-1-903071-28-1
Text © Bill Colegrave
Photography copyright Dillon Coleman and Antony Kitchin

A CIP catalogue record of this is available from the British Library

Cover and book design by Mousemat Design Ltd

Printed in Malta on behalf of Latitude Press Limited

CONTENTS

*Richard Burton, after his Nile expedition, was asked
whether he had now achieved his ambitions as an
explorer. He replied that he had not and 'fain would
find out the fountains of . . . Ganges and of Oxus'.*

2007 journey through
Tajikistan and Wakhan

Osh

KYRGYZSTAN

CHINA

Lake Kara Kul

TAJIKISTAN

AFGHANISTAN

Murghab

Vomar Roshan –
Confluence of
Bartang and
Panj Oxus

Wakhan
Corridor

Sarhad

Ishkashim

PAKISTAN

6704

Karl Marx Peak
6723

AFGH

Langar

Qala Panj

Wakhan River

5621

Wakhan Corridor

Ishaksem

Hindu Kush

PAKISTAN

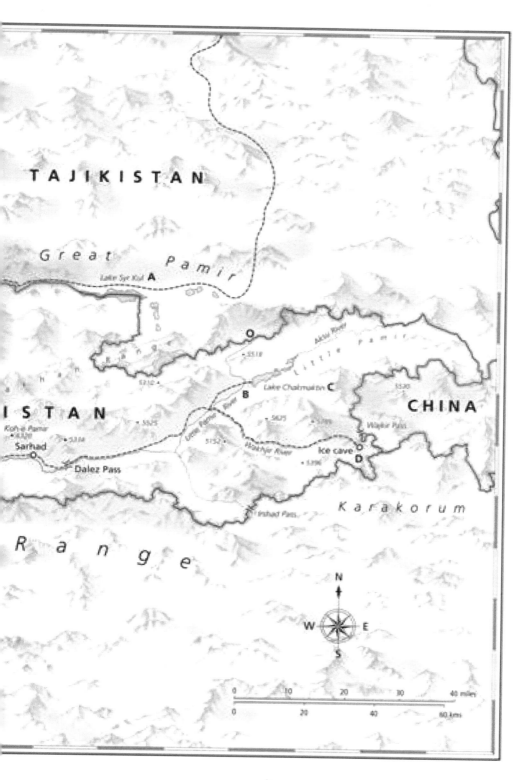

TAJIKISTAN

Great Pamir

Lake Syr Kul A

Little Pamir

Aksu River

CHINA

Lake Chakmaktin C

B

Koh-e Pamir

Sarhad

Dalez Pass

Wakjir Pass

Ice cave

D

Karakorum

Range

N
W   E
S

0   10   20   30   40 miles

0   20   40   60 kms

CHAPTER ONE

The Lure of the Oxus

It was best to appear to be usefully occupied when the history master arrived, so I picked a book out of the shelves. I chose Matthew Arnold, thinking he was the author of *Tom Brown's School Days*. Instead I found myself reading an epic poem of battle in places with fairy-tale names like High Tartary, and the River Oxus. Tartary is not a place or a country to be found on any map, and Oxus will only now be found on old ones. But these were names that bore with them the scent of adventure and mystery. I had learned something of Goths, Vandals, Mongols, or collectively, Tartars, but knew nothing of the dark expanse of map they occupied. High Tartary, a heart within the darkness, was no more real to me than Liliput, but it conjured the ghosts of the Great Khan and woolly mammoth. The seeds of a fascination were sown that day, which is when this journey really began.

Twenty six years later, in July 1990, I was lying in my bath. It was a scenic bath, elevated on a dais, so that one could look out over the fields and woods of Berkshire. Hot water, soft bubbles, fine views, and a glass of Tio Pepe to hand; fertile ground for planning a little adventure. The beautiful Soraya, soon to be my wife, brought me the phone. It was a man I didn't know, who wanted information about Tajikistan, the most obscure of the then collapsing Soviet Union's soft underbelly states. We talked for a while as I soaked and I told him the little I knew, and mentioned my fascination with the Oxus River (now generally known as Amu Darya), which is the country's southern border with Afghanistan. He was going there to investigate opportunities for the tourist trade. He talked like a traveller though; I felt we could get on, so I asked if I could join him.

Five days later we were together in Moscow.

Out of a drab, bustling crowd at Sheremetyeva Airport emerged a dapperly dressed Russian lady with orange blonde hair, whom my companion claimed to be his wife, though she did not seem so certain about this. She had an air of confidence and organisation amid the general disorder. She took us to one of Stalin's massive 1920s constructions, by then being used as a hotel.

She was a stiletto through the flesh of tortuous Russian bureaucracy. She came up to my room with an old mechanical typewriter, and with the ease of a KGB agent peeled off the flimsy visa that had been glued to my passport pages. She carefully added typed lines of Cyrillic script, which were a whole range of new destinations I wanted to visit, including Dushanbe, capital of Tajikistan. When she had finished she pasted it back and handed me the passport.

A day later at six the next morning I was in Dushanbe having my hair cut. The barber's chair was in the middle of a fruit and vegetable market, always the best place to visit first in a new city, especially in Central Asia, since the traders are usually smiling, approachable and helpful. As it was early, there were still high piles of root vegetables, aubergines, tomatoes, and industrial-sized bunches of beans, tied together with their own stalks. Although noisy and bustling, transactions were relaxed and accompanied by easy talk. The barber chatted to me throughout my cut, unconcerned that I had no idea what he was saying.

That evening we were in the back of an old military truck with a group of young Tajik men, travelling southeast on the dirt roads. We squeezed together on wooden benches, lengthways in the back of the open truck, protected only by a black tarpaulin cover. The Tajiks were still very nervous of Russians, and Russian authority. Some were avoiding or trying to avoid army service. They taught us the Russian for "I am an Estonian" in case we were stopped by police. Estonians were known not to speak Russian and they thought that the ruse might divert further inquiries. Twice there were roadblocks but each time the enquiries seemed to be all about the vehicle rather than its occupants.

Much of the fifteen-hour journey was by night, and the only view was through a slit at the back of the covering; brake lights reflecting in pools, on the rutted tracks, and patches of snow in heathery hollows. Eventually I dozed, and woke to a spring blue morning in some of the most glorious country in Asia; a succession of shallow valleys, like multi-coloured Scottish grouse moors, with velveteen undulating faces, looking so soft that one might pick them up and stroke them. Whole mountainsides were covered in a patchwork of wild flowers and herbs, neatly assorted into colour groups: mauve, yellow, white, purple.

By mid-morning we were in a narrow defile following a stream, bouncing downhill; iron-red rocks sparkling through milk-foamed glacial melt. As we reached the base of the valley our stream buried itself in a steel grey river, a hundred, maybe two hundred metres wide, held by sheer rock cliffs on the far side.

This was the Oxus, the river of romance and legend; the river of Sohrab and Rustum, the river Alexander crossed one way and Babur and the Moghuls the other; the river that gave Robert Byron the title for Road to Oxiana even though he never reached it; the river that beguiled Wilfred Thesiger, though he never saw it; the mainly un-navigable river that remains today, as it was in the 19th century, the frontier between two halves of Asia; the river whose "waters, descending from the Roof of the World, tell of forgotten peoples and whisper secrets of unknown lands" (George Nathaniel Curzon). The cliffs on the other side made up the northern tip of Afghanistan.

I stopped the truck briefly, to live the moment; my first sight of the Oxus: to paddle in its fast, cold, water rushing from the high Pamir Mountains. This was just another river for my Tajik companions, but for me it was a private ambition achieved; one of those moments of chest-tightening pleasure that is often the reward of an adventure.

We found a small village and guest house where we could rest

"Where is the loo?", we asked the Russian interpreter.

He repeated the question to the Tajik, who then translated again, to the villagers. A mumbled monosyllabic reply in Tajik was translated back into Russian and then to us in English: "Everywhere" was the answer.

After a breakfast of flat bread and onions we continued upstream, east and then south, along the Oxus. All day we followed the mighty Oxus in its prime. Over half way between its source in the Pamir and its eventual exhaustion in the Kizil Kum deserts, it has assimilated all its major contributaries; here it was at its maximum power, driving Afghanistan apart from its northern neighbours.

The Oxus is a river in reverse; it was reputed to start with a bang at the Ice Cave source at the farthest eastern end of the Wakhan Corridor and ends with a whimper in the desert. It rises on the 'Roof of the World', the mountainous plateau of the Pamir, which is the geographical heart of Asia. The Pamir Mountains cover almost the whole of the Gorno-Badakshan region of Tajikistan, plus the Wakhan Corridor, which is the finger of north-eastern Afghanistan that reaches out into the mountains north of Pakistan to touch western China.

The mysterious Wakhan is the geographical hero of this tale. Eight hunded years ago it may have been Marco Polo's conduit to Cathay and later that of the Portuguese Benjamin Goez, who was sent by his fellow Jesuit monks in 1607 to try to rediscover the same route. During the 17th century the opening of sea routes ended European interest in transcontinental travel in Asia for more than two hundred years and the Wakhan was forgotten until the days of the Great Game gave it an unexpected flash of notoriety as the only place where at any time the British and Tsarist Russian empires ever confronted each other in Asia. Already one of the most tortuous places on earth to access, it was then further closed to all outside contact when the newly created Soviet Union sealed all its northern frontiers and soon afterwards Mao Tse Tung's new

China clamped the eastern door uncompromisingly shut. During the next several decades the Wakhan was less travelled by outsiders than the moon. It reverted to being a high altitude cul de sac on the very outer limits of geography.

After it leaves Wakhan the Oxus becomes for several hundred kilometres successively the border between Afghanistan and Tajikistan, and then Afghanistan and Uzbekistan. Crossing between Uzbekistan and Turkmenistan, it then turns north on its long journey to the inland Aral Sea. However the waters have been diverted and diminished by the depredations of Uzbek irrigation channels, and it no longer has the strength to reach the Sea.

It is unlike other great rivers such as the Mississippi, Ganges or Nile. These are rivers that irrigate and supply; rivers that are used for transport and communication; rivers that are the heart of the life of their countryside. The Oxus is none of these things. It is more of a barrier than a conduit, more of a danger than a boon. It is a Moses of a river, a river that divides, pushing regions apart It is a true border between cultures and countries. From time to time the surrounding cliffs retreat and the river spreads out in gentler mood, even creating the occasional sandy beach, but there are no boats, no fishing piers, no waterside houses, no bathers, only the lonely watchtowers which the Russians built as a gesture to control the flow of contraband, such as heroin, across the borders along the upper Oxus.

I was due to be back in London very soon. Khorog, five hours up river, was reputed to have an airport, and I hoped I could use that to return to Dushanbe. When we found it, it was just a flat strip by the roadside, with a control tower, and waiting area. There were no flights. My companion had gone back northwards with the vehicle and drivers to seek other potential tourism opportunities.

Then news came that a plane was due to land. After a few hours of waiting, bored and hungry, it finally arrived, and collected twenty or more passengers, who seemed to have materialized from surrounding trees. The bad news was that there was no more room on-board, and anyway the plane was going on to Osh in Kyrghizia, a thousand kilometres west of where I needed to be.

I had no right to be upset but I was; I stomped around the plane kicking the ground in frustration. Apparently the pilot saw me remonstrating with an airport official, and came to talk to me via an interpreter. An animated conversation followed, after which they took me aside and told me, quietly, that if I would give the pilot twenty dollars he would divert the flight to Dushanbe.

Soon I was aboard. There was no room in the passenger compartment, so I flew the whole way standing behind the co-pilot's seat. For reasons I never understood, we flew first to somewhere that they said was near the China border to the East, where we landed by another small river, on a rust coloured track; it was much colder and the altimeter was showing over 13,000 ft. Eventually we took off for Dushanbe. The plane stayed there all day, so I have no idea what happened to the twenty passengers who had expected to be flown to Osh, but had instead been brought with me to Dushanbe, hijacked for a twenty dollar bribe.

My ambition to reach the river had been achieved, but this had only deepened my desire to explore the river further, and a renewed ambition to find its source, and to understand something of the unknown places it flowed through, and of where it was born.

This book is an exploration of the river and the story of this search for its source. The Oxus had lured and seduced 19th-century travellers such as George Curzon (later Viceroy of India) Captain Francis Younghusband, and earlier, Marco Polo and 7th-century Chinese Buddhist pilgrims. Many had set out with the intention of solving the mystery of the source of the great river in the High Pamir. By the end of the 19th century four rival theories had been proposed. The supporters of the various theories had fought their various corners in print and in lecture halls particularly in the Royal Geographical Society. The advocates included, amongst others, a Naval Lieutenant, John Wood, who for many years in the mid 19th century had been thought to have discovered in 1838 the true source at Lake Syr Kul on what is now the Tajik/Afghan border. Following Wood more than forty years later came an Indian scout, known as 'the Mirza', two French explorers, several Russians and the British traveller hunting team of Colonel Trotter and the Earl of Dunmore and Sir Francis Younghusband.

Then Lord Curzon, following his 1895 expedition, announced to the world that he had found the source, which he alone had seen: an Ice Cave, in a fairy-tale setting, at the conjunction of the great mountain ranges of Asia, at the far end of Afghanistan's Wakhan Corridor, at the very point where the five great mountain chains of Central Asia merge.

The strident Curzon was only somewhat timidly challenged by those of his competitors who were still alive in 1895. Nevertheless at the end of the 19th century there were four claimants for the true 'fountain of Oxus': (marked as A,B,C,D on map on pages 8/9)

A. Lake Syr Kul (Lt John Wood)

B. Sarhad or Little Pamir River (the 'Mirza' and others)

C. Lake Chakmaktin (Dunmore, Trotter)

D. The Ice Cave (Curzon)

But the 20th century saw the end of the Great Game standoff between British India and the Tzarist Empire that had motivated much of the earlier exploration and also the clamp of iron and bamboo curtains around most of Central Asia. So the Oxus issue remained unresolved, or forgotten for more than a hundred years. As far as I knew, no one had visited all possible sources of the river to answer the question that had intrigued the Victorian public, as well as the explorers themselves.

In July 2007, seventeen years after that first tantalising glimpse of the Oxus I set out, with two new companions, to do just that. Our initial objective was to find Curzon's Ice Cave, and then to determine whether this or one of the others was the true source of the river. But there was a fifth possible solution that had proposed itself from the study of many maps. It seemed to be such an unlikely solution that I had hardly even discussed it before departing. However it was a theory was was later to play an important part in our story.

11th century Persian poet Abolqasem Ferdowsi popularised the story of Sohrab and Rustum in his epic Shahnameh

CHAPTER TWO

Sohrab and Rustum

There is a story from the folklore of Persia and Afghanistan, which invests the Oxus with the romance of Camelot. It came to Victorian Britain as a haunting epic poem by Matthew Arnold. It was this that I had chanced upon in my history master's study many years earlier. It is a story that has brought pride, and a sense of tradition to generations of Afghans and Iranians.

The poem was quoted by Curzon in his *Pamirs and the Source of the Oxus* and by Sir Henry Rawlinson, in his 1872 Royal Geographical Society paper that sought to explain the fascination of his contemporaries with the river.

It was probably in the minds of other memorable tellers of Central Asian tales and journeys such as Younghusband, and more recently Sir Fitzroy MacLean and Peter Hopkirk. It is also the silent reference point for Khaled Hosseini's *The Kite Runner*.

Real dates and places have long since been forgotten in the telling and retelling of the story, and the heroes are claimed by all tribes and nations as their own. Rustum was the leader in battle, and inspiration of the peoples of Oxiana, be they Persians, Pathans or Afghans. He was the military talisman, the leader under whose command all campaigns prevailed. He was the warrior who aroused the combatants when morale was low: an Afghan Sir Lancelot; Richard, Coeur de Lion, and Leonidas of Thermopylae all rolled into one. He was only twenty when his reputation was made.

This was a time when the fighting between the central Asian people was a way of life. The traditional battle ground was between the Farsi-speaking southerners, and the invading hordes of Mongols and their descendants from the north. Little has changed over the centuries, as even then, as now, the invaders were comparatively the well-armed and organised armies, while the defenders were seen as the guerrilla fighters.

Political and social power was to be won on the battlefield. Fighting followed the Afghan version of the rules of chivalry, which demanded respect and help for the vanquished, with support for the widows and families of the slain.

Late one year Rustum crossed the Oxus with a few companions to try to discover, from informants, the strength and intentions of the Tartar armies. The snows came early and closed the passes out of the valley; they were trapped for the winter. Rustum was saved from starvation or capture by the inhabitants of a village; there he and his small retinue were allowed to overwinter. He spent the long, cold nights with the beautiful daughter of the headman of the village. When spring came and the snows receded, he was again allowed to travel. Rustum returned south not knowing that he had fathered a son in the village.

The son was called Sohrab and grew into a clone of his illustrious father with all his courage and skill. He had just one ambition; to find and prove himself to his missing father, but had no idea where, or how, to find him. By the age of eighteen he was already known and admired in the army of Peran Wisa, the Tartar chieftain, so much so that he had the ear of the general himself.

Peran Wisa had brought his army to face the Afghans yet again, on the banks of the Oxus. As the sun rose over the camp, Sohrab went to Peran Wisa, whose own tent was pitched on the low banks of the slow flowing summer river. He was awake and planning battle, but Sohrab sought to change his mind. "Let the armies rest today", he asked. "Let me instead give challenge, man to man, to the champion of the Afghans in single-handed combat. If I win my fame will spread and surely someday the great Rustum will hear and find a way to meet his son". Peran Wisa would not agree at first; he feared for the health of the headstrong, fearless young Sohrab; but he also knew that nothing would halt him in his search for his father, so he granted his wish.

Peran Wisa addressed his squadrons. Sohrab, he told them, was to fight alone for them that day. The Tartar champion would stand in the stead of all the Tartar armies and hazard his life for theirs. Centuries of tradition required that the challenge be taken up by the Afghans; the shame of refusal allowed no other course. Every man knew then that a life that day would be sacrificed to save his own.

The Afghans knew of Sohrab's peerless talents and achievements; they had no champion to match the young man with the wild stag's foot and the lion's heart. But as they wondered how to meet the challenge, news came of the arrival in camp of Rustum, still the finest swordsman and most admired warrior in all of Oxiana.

They went to Rustum and asked him to accept the challenge. Rustum refused and told them to find another, as his days were done. He knew of young Sohrab's fame, and wished he had a son like him to bear his mantle, and help him in his older years, as he had to help his own old father now. But the Afghan King persuaded him that refusal would be considered to be a surrender of his reputation. He agreed to fight but only on condition that he did so anonymously. The armies moved from camp and formed themselves in two long lines on the banks of the great river to witness the combat.

Father and son closed on each other, swords drawn, watched by the two silent armies.

Rustum was bemused and disturbed by his opponent's great skills, his bravado and youthfulness. Then as they tested and feinted with each other, there was something more; a hint of recognition, a familiarity that he couldn't place. The seasoned fighter put it out of his mind, and answered his misgivings by hurling his spear at the nimble Sohrab, who saw it come and sprang aside. Sohrab flung his in turn, striking Rustum on the shield.

It deflected the spear, and the father took up his club, a famous weapon that reputedly only he could wield. Again Sohrab easily evaded the strike, but stood and waited for Rustum; also pondering his opponent.

Rustum now was angry, and rekindled his son's own fire with his taunts. Sohrab shouted that he was the son of Rustum and soon Rustum would hear of his exploits and be proud. His adversary answered that everyone knew that Rustum had no son, only a daughter, happily far away in safer lands. But there was a questioning and uncertainty in his voice that shook the younger man.

In that instant of doubt, and surprise Sohrab lost his concentration and let down his guard; it was barely perceptible, but just enough for his father's fighting brain to sense the chance and make the fatal thrust. Rustum's sword met Sohrab's breast and felled him. As it did so the father saw on his son's neck the lapis amulet he had given to Sohrab's mother on parting twenty years before.

It stopped him dead, forced his breath from him, and he knew. He knew with a hurt that rent his soul and paralysed his senses. He roared a father's pain across the plain and clasped his dying son in his arms.

For brief, impossibly valuable minutes, they lay together on the sand, united but irreparably torn apart. In those few minutes a whole lifetime's bond between father and child was compressed: love, hope, pride and the terrible recognition of hopelessness.

With the final words of his dying son, Rustum heard tell, for a few precious moments, of his son's childhood, his short, but lifelong search for his father, his single-minded ambition, and the exploits that had brought him to this end.

Then: '…. on the bloody sands Sohrab lay dead
And the great Rustum drew his horseman's cloak
Down o'er his face and sate by his dead son.'

For most poets, or dramatists that would be the end; what more could be added? But Arnold wanted to show something else, that this was a tragedy with no villains, only heroes. Death had fulfilled their lives. The drama had ennobled the participants, and the spectators, even the lands they came from; they could all be proud.

To explain this, Arnold used the metaphor of the great river itself flowing now, with enhanced grandeur:

> But the majestic River floated on,
> Out of the misty hum of that low land,
> into the frosty starlight, and there moved,
> Rejoicing through the hushed Chorasmian waste
> Under the solitary moon: — he flowed
> Right for the polar star, past Orange,
> Brimming, bright, and large: then sands begin
> To hem his watery march, and dam his streams,
> And split his currents; that for many a league
> The shorn and parcelled Oxus strains along
> Through beds of sand and matted rushy isles —
> Oxus, forgetting the bright speed he had
> In his high mountain-cradle in Pamere,
> A foiled circuitous wanderer: — till at last
> The longed-for dash of waves is heard, and wide
> His luminous home of waters opens, bright
> And tranquil, from whose floor the new-bathed stars
> Emerge, and shine upon the Aral Sea
> (Matthew Arnold, 'Sohrab and Rustum')

These lines have reverberated in my head for years and more than anything else led me to the Wakhan.

Matthew Arnold had never been to Central Asia and may have had little idea what the Oxus was like but he created in his story images that were to draw travellers for more than a century to seek the outlaw romance of the Pamir and Afghanistan, the most invaded but least conquerable country on earth.

I needed to see the 'majestic river' floating on and find 'its cradle in the high Pamere'.

CHAPTER THREE

An Iranian Daughter and the Very Centre of Asia

The speed visit in 1990 was not strictly the first time I had seen the river. There had been previous journeys, skirmishes in the area which just added to the sense of mystery of the Wakhan. The first time was long before, when I had flown over the Oxus in 1977, on my way from Tashkent, Uzbekistan to Kabul on a mission, partly for a friend. It started when I was walking down Holland Park Avenue, London one Saturday morning in April that year, and I saw an old girl friend. She was an attractive and entertaining Australian nurse. She looked to be many months pregnant.

The father of the child turned out to be one Dr Hossein Davoudi, the then Iranian Ambassador to Kabul. She had taken a trip back to Australia and on the return journey had met, and become the Head of Household, (or in reality, girlfriend) of the forty eight year old unmarried Davoudi. Their relationship was unknown to his government, then still under the leadership of the Shah and the Pahlavi family. He would have been instantly dismissed, or worse, had it been discovered that he had a western girlfriend, which is why she had returned to London to have the child, which was born a few weeks later.

I visited mother and baby, and was concerned that the father wasn't there, and had not contacted them yet. Since I was planning to travel east at the time she asked me to visit him in Afghanistan on the way. A few days later, I was in the long marble salons of the Iranian Embassy in Kabul. I handed Davoudi the picture of his only child. I did so with some care, so that the guards would have no hint of what was going on, as I had the strictest instructions not to allow anyone else to know the real purpose of the visit. He looked at the photograph and handed it back without a word. Although we then spent several days together, it was never mentioned again between us, though I do know that he became a dutiful father to his daughter.

Afghanistan in the days before the Russians came in 1979, was a much more travelled place than it is today. It was frequently part of the hippy trail east, and it was not unusual for Europeans to drive through Iran and Afghanistan on the way to India. But to the north of the Oxus the countries were virtually unknown.

These were my first days in Central Asia. Every sight and smell was novel, and alluring. I walked the streets of a peaceful, but soon to be turbulent, Kabul. I wandered amongst the rice mounds, spice sacks, exotic woods, caged chickens and foraging hounds. I weaved between the hanging carcasses of the hillside meat markets, drained by a central gutter that seemed to be home to all of Asia's flies. I sat and watched the traders; one moment listless, and dozing in the sun, and next animatedly selling offal, cow heads and feet. I bought Kuchi nomad dresses with pressed silver ornaments and woollen rosettes, which I thought to use as wall decorations at home. I met an American girl, fresh out Stanford University in California, who had married an Afghan classmate and moved to Kabul, only to discover that she was wife number two and could not leave, as her passport had been taken from her.

I flew in a tiny aircraft under the black storm clouds through the mountains to Bamian, accompanied by a solo Christian nun. The only sign of military activity was a few variously dressed soldiers marching out of step across the airstrip as we tried to land. The huge Buddhas, (later to be destroyed by the Taliban), still dominated Bamian. One could climb up onto their three metre high feet, and wind up a long stair to stand by their faces. I slept in a guest yurt on the hill above the small town. It belonged to a shepherd farmer, who also offered one of his young women relations to keep me company for the night.

Hossein Davoudi quickly became a friend, and also an ally, in my ambitions to explore the country. He was an expert in both the political and natural history of Afghanistan. We made plans for a visit to Nuristan together. He was determined to get his friend, Afghan President Mohammed Daoud Khan, to send a detachment of soldiers with us. All this however was to be thwarted by the Russian-inspired deposition of the President, and subsequent occupation of the country during in 1979, and by Dr Davoudi's inevitable loss of office not long after the fall of the Shah in the same year.

It was not only my friend's baby that sent me to Afghanistan. The romance had been sown a long time before, by Matthew Arnold, and burnished subsequently by others. Eric Newby's *A Short Walk in the Hindu Kush*, for instance, is the story of his adventure in Nuristan, and the starting point for so many love affairs with Central Asia. Newby was working in the family business in Bond Street, sewing garments, when he impulsively telegraphed his friend Hugh Carless, a British diplomat in Peru; 'Shall we travel to Nuristan June?' Carless had lived and worked in Kabul, and had enthused the young Newby with the possibilities for exploration. Nuristan is in the north west of Afghanistan and is home to many of the major peaks of the Hindu Kush. Newby was an amateur traveller in the tradition of Peter Fleming, brother of Ian, and well known for his adventures in Brazil, Manchuria and Chinese Turkestan. Newby had none of Fleming's self importance as a writer; instead he recorded his adventures with self-deprecating humour, which is what makes *A Short Walk* the classic that it is. Their plan, which almost succeeded, was to make the first recorded ascent of Mir Samir, the highest mountain in the range, but they set out with just a hand-drawn map, little idea of what they would encounter, and no experience of mountaineering.

Equally intriguing was Robert Byron's *Road to Oxiana*. Byron was the poet's great great grandson. The Byronic tradition revered Classical Greece, and all its works, as the romantic foundation for European culture; his namesake and descendant had just the same reverence for things classical, but moved the focus of attention further East.

For Byron Oxiana is Afghanistan. Transoxiana is the wild unknown across the river. Both were prizes worth the travel. He and his friend Christopher, about whom we learn little, travelled across Europe, the Middle East and Iran mainly in their vehicle 'the charcoal burner' in order to find Oxiana. He writes with a young man's certainty, about taste and style in all matters cultural, but particularly about architecture. He feels free to pass judgement on everything built between Beirut and Kabul. When they finally reach Afghanistan he gushes over the Minaret of Jam near Herat, but derides the colossal naiveté of the Bamian Buddhas. Byron came from an era in which there was a strong mutual respect between Muslim and Christian cultures, which were seen as complementing, rather than competing with each other. Baghdad, Istanbul and Damascus were as desirable destinations as Rome or Paris.

Neither Newby nor Byron ever got near the Wakhan, or even reached the Oxus, but they were lured by the drama of the region. Their great skill as writers was that even today, they still manage to take us with them, as co-equal conspirators, in the discovery of Central Asia.

Then there was a picture: one image from Galen Rowell's 'Mountains of the Middle Kingdom'. It showed a scene of such huge scale, that in comparison, any European landscape was like that of a doll's house. It was a yellow ochre sand-dune, sweeping out of a spring green carpet. There was a tiny figure at the bottom left, a lone horseman travelling across the landscape; it was so small, it might have been the artist's signature. This was my first, and for a very long time, only glimpse of the soft beauty of a Pamir basin. That image, like the words of Matthew Arnold, was to live with me for many years and to tempt me, finally, to the Roof of the World.

It was the opening of the Khunjerab Pass which connected Chinese Xinjiang to Pakistan that was one catalyst for my next journey in the area.

I read about it in a one-line news item in the corner of *The Times* and determined to go there.

The road leading to the pass, the Karakorum Highway, was a triumph of years of battle against the crumbling new rock of the Karakorum. Although subject to almost daily blocking landslides in the rainy times of the year, it did finally provide a vehicle route north from the populated areas of Pakistan to the Chinese border, opening some access between the subcontinent and its northern neighbour. It became the only regularly usable conduit across the Karakorum/Himalaya massif of China/Afghanistan between the Khyber Pass and Nepal.

The other catalyst was reading Wilfred Thesiger's *The Marsh Arabs*, as brilliantly evocative a travel book as has ever been written. It covers his two long sojourns in the 1950s with the Madan in the marshes south of Basra, Iraq. Every word of the book is about the marshes except for this one tantalising paragraph:

> 'I had left in the last week of July. It was now an early afternoon in February. Seven months later; it seemed longer. In that time I had crossed high passes through the snows of the Hindu Kush to see the cold blue Lake of Korumbar where the Chitral River rises; I had looked out over the Wakhand from the Boroghil Pass and seen the glint in the distance which was the Oxus; I had slept on the glaciers at the foot of Tirich Mir, and in the dark, verminous houses among the mulberry orchards, where last of the Black Kaffirs lived on the borders of Nuristan'.

The *'glint in the distance'* certainly was not the Oxus as there is no place on the Afghanistan/Pakistan border from which the river would be visible; it is at all times in a deep valley or steep gorge; Wilfred would have had to have been in a helicopter to see the river. But he had the same sense of history and longing to see the river, and it would have been tempting to persuade himself that he had done so.

I recruited Inki, the wife of my good friend, the Norwegian shipowner Johann Reksten, and his sister to go to Pakistan and try to travel the new road and cross into China, with a view to continuing to Lhasa, Tibet. The plan was to go from North Pakistan into China and then find our way eastwards into Tibet. We left Islamabad and went via Peshawar and up the Afghan border country, then populated by a million or more refugees from the Russian occupation. Some were living in camps, but most had just adopted places on the roadside in fields. We passed through Swat and then Dir in Pakistan's North West Frontier Province, where my two female companions had to hide under rugs in the back of our 4x4 for fear of being seen improperly escorted. The men in the villages carried Kalashnikovs; these were the tribal areas and the writ of Islamabad Government did not carry much weight, so power was in the hands of local commanders. We crossed the Lowari Top Pass into Chitral, the north-eastern tip of geographic Pakistan. Lowari has more than a hundred switchbacks, almost all visible together from the summit of the pass as a rolling ripple of roadway. The route north to Chitral is then a succession of deep valleys with no more than a handkerchief of sky visible between the peaks. Chitral is the north westernmost corner of what was claimed as British India. It was an occasional garrison town in the time of British India, but usually under the control of the Mir or his family, who were not always friends of the occupiers of much of the subcontinent. It was never truly part of the Empire, any more than the rest of the Princely States and Tribal Areas.

It has a red brick fort overlooking it and is all but surrounded by an 180 degree bend of the upper River Indus. In 1986 it was little changed from the 19th century... a few guest houses, a market and narrow hillside streets above the river valley. The men all wear warm grey-brown or white shalwar kameez and the distinctive Chitrali cap, which looks like a thick elephant sock that has been rolled up and pulled onto their heads; the women, even those working the fields, wear swirling dresses of bright yellows, reds and greens and in terms of dress have few of the social inhibitions of their more retiring compatriots elsewhere in the country. The regular form of transport is donkey.

We left Chitral on a fearsome road. "Many peoples they fall off", said Kachu, our happy and resourceful guide. The vehicle often had to make three point turns to get round corners. Sometimes the crumbling rock road was replaced by slatted wood supports attached to the mountainside, through which the long drop to the Indus or valley floor was visible.

We camped on the upper reaches of the Indus. Food was the ubiquitous rice and whatever was available to give flavour. One lucky time this was six tiny trout caught by Kachu on his collapsible fly rod that he kept under his flowing white shirt. He diverted us off the track into the hills to the south and found a fast silver stream; almost immediately he had the little fish taking his line. That night we had a cabin on the hillside above the Indus; just two brick rooms with a central fireplace. It was private luxury compared with previous nights and we gloried in the sliding grandeur of the young Indus way below us as the evening sun burned pinks and oranges into its sleekness. Over the river and further over the extended eastern arms of the Hindu Kush was the Boroghil Pass, and the way into the Wakhan, which we presumed to be inaccessible as it was thought that the Russians had landmined the access points. Our peace was disturbed when a group of very senior officers from the Pakistan army arrived expecting to use our cabin for the night. Having seen almost no one for two days this was a surprise, and resulted in a momentary stand-off, but such is the tradition of hospitality in the area that soon we were companions and sharing not only the rooms, but the six little fish that before seemed to be small fare for four but now was more than enough for twelve .

We remained south and west of the Wakhan and reached Chinese Turkestan via Gilgit and after a few days of struggle through the landslides of the Karakorum Highway, the Khunjerab Pass. The pass is marked by a small cairn. It was five o'clock on a cold, airless morning at 15,500 feet. We were standing there at the very centre of Asia. To the east were the Himalayas, behind was the Karakorum, to the west the Hindu Kush. To the north west was the Pamir and I thought, probably imagined, that I could see a defile up which, surely, was the route into the Wakhan. In front the wide open space was Xingiang and Chinese Turkestan. It was an extraordinary and special place to stand with the whole of Central Asia apparently at one's feet. At that moment the determination to make it into Wakhan someday was made real.

CHAPTER FOUR

Contending with Demons

It was the defeat of the Taliban government by US and allied forces in 2003, even though it was followed by civil war in many parts of the country, which created the opportunity of getting to Wakhan more easily, since there was now no government authority which had good reasons to deny the right to travel. So the time had come to go and find our river.

I needed to find good guides, porters and support, so I consulted the few people that I knew of, who were familiar with North East Afghanistan. Eventually I settled for a team leader who had been recruited via agents in Faisabad. Although they had no experience of Wakhan itself, they were Afghans, knew the Badakshan area very well, and seemed capable of recruiting everything we needed, such as horses, horsemen, cooks and supplies in advance.

Although I'd studied the maps in detail, and as many other sources as I could find, I was still troubled by the thought that we'd meet some impenetrable barrier that would halt our progress, and bring our exploration to a humiliating failure. I'd had email conversations with the remarkable John Mock, Reader in Central Asian Languages at the University of California and the only Westerner, that I knew of, who spoke the language of the people of the Wakhan. He had traversed Wakhan with his travel writer wife, Kimberley O'Neil, in 2004 and he was keen to set my mind at rest on the issue.

I recruited two companions for the expedition from amongst friends who were likely to be interested. Inevitably there had been many more potential travellers when I first promoted the idea, but most of them eventually dropped out. The two who stayed were Anthony Kitchin, and Dillon Coleman. Anthony was an old friend, a farmer from Sligo in Ireland, and always game for an adventure; he hardly asked a question about where we were going, or what we would be doing. He just sent his passport for the many awkward visas to be obtained, and turned up at London's Heathrow Airport ready to run. Although he knew little in advance of our objectives he did have knowledge of two subjects that were to be valuable to us, farming and geology. Anthony had a happy, self-deprecating sense of humour, even in times of crisis, or when he himself was not feeling good or in awkward conditions.

Dillon Coleman, an American from Raleigh, North Carolina, contacted me by email, having read of my plan on a website. From the moment I read his first email, he was very clearly the right companion for the journey. He sent me his CV to confirm his pedigree; it read like a CIA cover, created by John le Carré. He had lived and worked for two years in Afghanistan as well as in several other countries in the region. His deep knowledge of the politics and history of Central Asia was much more up to date than mine; he even spoke a little of some of the useful languages we would encounter, such as Russian and Farsi. I had no hesitation in asking him to join us.

He took much longer to agree, and examined my plans in detail, and one after another asked all the questions, and raised all the issues that I should have already considered, and pretended that I had. Without his careful review, we would have made many more mistakes. Dillon, the American, at all times looked like the embodiment of the true 19th-century English traveller, straight-backed on his horse, well turned out, and seemingly confident. Whatever the difficult or dangerous moments

Dillon's demeanour, unlike mine, never outwardly changed.

All boded well, until, just a week or two before the scheduled departure, when I chanced across a book in my library, that twenty years before had been another foundation of my interest in the Wakhan. *The Trail of Marco Polo*, by the American explorer Jean Bowie Shor, told of her journey there in 1948. Jean and her husband, Franc, had travelled from Kabul via Kunduz, and then into, and through, the whole Wakhan.

If they had not branched off to take the Wakhjir Pass into China, and then south to Hunza, they would have followed an identical journey to the one I had planned.

The bath is an excellent place to ruminate over a travel book, so I took Jean Shor there, expecting some new insights, ideas, and no additional worries. How wrong I was. I wish I had never picked it up. Suddenly, all the fears that for months I had pushed to the back of my mind, were rekindled again.

Within twenty minutes I was jumping out out of the bath, certain that it was all over. There was no way I could go, I would have to call Anthony and Dillon with some fanciful excuse for cancelling the whole expedition.

Two days after leaving Ishkashem Shor writes:

"we pressed on, over terrifying trails to Nurss. At some points the path was literally tacked to the cliff by branches and sticks jammed into the rock wall, and covered by brush and rocks piled on top. This is a type of construction that is common in the Wakhan and elsewhere in the Pamir…It is disconcerting to look down through the road and see daylight.

The trail east of Boroghil rose almost straight up, over paths of treacherous shifting shale and around sheer rock chimneys. We crossed our first pass at 13,400 ft, and thereafter we were rarely below that level and often far above it. Until then we had been little troubled by anoxemia for our climb had been gradual. But after we left Boroghil, and approached the Pamir plateau, every unusual exertion left me gasping.

The trail clung to the cliffs by rock fingertips, and here again we could look down through the rocks to slender rivers twisting far below. In many places we were forced to dismount and lead our horses up steeply pitched, sliding rubble, or around hairpin bends where one miss-step would be the last. At times the trail was so narrow that had I extended my elbows one would have bumped rock and the other tip would have been out over airy space."

That was everything that I did not want to hear, and a good bit more. These were the predicaments that I was not ready to meet.

It is hard to reconcile vertigo with a fascination for the mountains but I had always had a fear of heights, so much so that as a child, I would wake up in the night fearfully convinced that I had been standing exposed on a tower or eerie ledge. I still have these nightmares, and so consequently, every journey I plan is as fraught with background worries about what would happen if I was left stranded, incapable of achieving a traverse that appeared to be so simple for others. Other sufferers of vertigo will know that it not just a matter of the fear of falling, so much as an emptiness and powerlessness that overtakes the psyche in an instant; suddenly the mountain seems to be beside you, and on top of you, actively pressing you out, into the void. The imbalance of forces becomes so crucial, that you can think of nothing else; it paralyses mind and limbs. My own problem came to a head on one of my earlier approaches to the Wakhan, in 1988, in a little valley, the Shimshal, in the Karakorum mountains in North Pakistan, close to the Chinese border. I had returned there with Inki Reksten, one of my companions from Khunjerab trip in 1986.

Inki was very beautiful, with big round blue eyes, straw-coloured hair and a wild happy smile. She was reckless and ambitious, and could afford to indulge her whims for travel and exploration. She had married young, and now in her mid 30s, she wanted to find a new focus. She had become a very keen mountaineer and was talking of trying to climb K2. So our 1988 expedition was in part preparation for her later more ambitious plans.

We met in Islamabad and, to plan the journey, recruited the help of our old friend Raja Changez Sultan, who managed to run Pakistan Tourism whilst also being a published poet, and respected artist. The three of us dined with Imran Khan, who was about to be brought back out of temporary retirement as Pakistan cricket captain; he and Changez all but decided to accompany us but instead we planned a later trip to the Deosai plains, a Pamir-like high altitude flatland not far from K2.

We set off the next day up the Karakorum Highway towards Hunza. The fabled mountain oasis of Hunza, often considered the inspiration of the Shangri La myth, is the home of a traditionally long living people. Their diet of fruit, particularly apricots and their kernels, is often cited as the reason for their longevity. In the 19th century Hunza was also the home of the Kanjuti bandits who were a scourge of even well defended expeditions trying to reach the Chinese border through the Karakorum. It would have been via Hunza that almost all the explorations into Pamir and northern Hindu Kush began. It guards the only direct route north..

Every traveller who arrives for the first time at this little haven in the hills is struck by its astonishing beauty, its chocolate box perfection. It is dominated by Rakaposhi mountain, which is the only major peak in the Karakorum that can be viewed almost from base to peak. Rakaposhi grows out of the gorge where the young black Indus runs; it rises up past the riparian villages, shaded by mountain birch and white mulberry, with little clusters of low, stone built houses with wooden doors, sometimes ornately carved, set in the walls. Above this the green-gold apple and apricot groves grow, then the tussocked, steep fields supporting goat and sheep. Further up, the trees and scrub die out, and the sheer black Karakorum rock rises another fifteen vertical kilometres to the sparkling white triangle of the 27,000 ft peak.

At the northern end of the Hunza valley the indomitable Baltit fort stands, allowing access and exit, or not, as the case might be. This for 150 years, had been the means of control, not only for the various Mirs of Hunza, over their pugnacious subjects, but also over all those who chose to try to take the route north. Control of the Baltit fort meant control of the whole area.

Our objective was to reach an isolated village, Shimshal, high above, and towards the long Hispar glacier to the west of Hunza. The team was just Inki, me, and two porters. The second night out we camped in a tent under a very unpleasant looking climb. It is hard for me to understand how stupid I could have been, not to have even considered the possibility that part of our proposed route might have been beyond my ability. Nevertheless it became rapidly clear that this would be the case.

I tried a practice climb directly up the face of the cliff that awaited us the next day; it did nothing but confirm my fears: crumpled with failure, I returned to the tent.

We argued into the night.

"I just can't do it, however much I want to", I said. "It's like your own demons, the snakes and avalanches that you have nightmares about". This was not a strong argument, since two years earlier she had faced her fears of snakes when we visited a snake farm in Bangkok together, but it was all I had by way of defence.

"Like it or not, you're coming with me. It is just a matter of pretending that you are somewhere else, and eventually, the adrenalin will buoy you up", she replied.

"The chances of me being buoyed up on the edge of a precipice are zero".

"OK, then keep your eyes closed and let the porters hold you on".

That sounded better, but not by much. I had lost the argument however, and agreed to try.

The next day we set off, and I was clearly trembling at the prospect. The route, compared with much rock climbing, or alpine mountaineering, was not technically hard, but there was no safety net, or margin for error of any sort. These were goat paths; goats like them, or maybe do not know any better, but humans do not, especially this one. There were no holds or ropes; just rock on one side, and fresh air on the other. The paths were thin ledges, on 75 degree faces, off which, it seemed all too easy to slip, and then there'd be nothing underneath but bare rocks or rocks and the rushing Shimshal river.

We started upwards. I saw little of the route, as I was being held up by one porter in front, and another behind, and my eyes were attached to the sheer rock on my right. I took a rest behind an available boulder, heaving with distress. We started again in the same pathetic crocodile line, whilst Inki was far ahead.

I should have simply carried on this way, without looking down. This is what Ranulph Fiennes was to do, to survive his extraordinarily courageous ascent of the Eiger, a few years later. He claims to suffer from the same problem as I do, and from the way he writes of his fears, he certainly does. But he was more determined than me. One of his solutions, in trying to overcome this fear, was to try for Everest, and finding that it did not really challenge him with 'fearful voids', decided to go instead for the Eiger, as he puts it, 'the daddy of all nasties'. This mountain terrifies me, even from inside the permanently sealed observation window, cut into the huge open face; it terrifies me even thinking of it, thousands of miles away. But somehow it also draws me in, and I have sat underneath it many times, usually after skiing with my younger daughter, Kara. I get fixated with it, examine every crack and distant crevice, and just wonder at the belly-jerking grandeur of the fearful face, not even daring to seriously contemplate the challenge that it presents. Fiennes must have done the same, and then learned to climb it, and did so. Almost every sentence of his story (in *Mad, Bad and Dangerous to Know*) spikes new fears, and trepidations, but the main lesson unfailingly is: 'do not look down'. "I was desperate to keep my mind busy with no tiny chink into which sheer terror could claw, then spread…".

On the climb to Shimshal I had not had the benefit of his counsel then, and felt alone and friendless amongst those who had no inkling of my hollow, leg-trembling horror.

So back in Surrey, still wet from my bath, book in hand, it all came rushing back to me; the cold, empty, anticipatory funk which Shor's words induced was not going away. I read it later, to Soraya, who was wholly sympathetic, and counselled caution. Sitting on the soft Surrey grass, there was a temptation to answer the question "Shall we go?" with "Let's not, but say we did". Nothing would be lost.

But we both knew really that it would; the years of anticipation, of reading and wondering, of poring over maps, imagining. All those hopes and ambitions would have been in vain, and a sham. So the only solution was to put it out of mind.

"At worst", she said, "you can go as far as possible and either deal with it, or come back". So that was decided.

Not a very promising posting for these Tajik border guards

CHAPTER FIVE

Back Door to Afghanistan

We still needed visas. The Afghanistan Embassy and Consulate in London, understandably a bit dishevelled, is in the same place it has been for 30 or more years, opposite the entrance to the Royal Geographical Society on Exhibition Road. There was no queue, and few officials, just a couple of friendly deskers who look excited at the idea of our Wakhan trip. Their attitude was refreshingly; 'hey, can we come along,' rather than the more usual reaction of 'why do you want to go to a war zone'?

The Tajik visas were more difficult. The proposed route required entry to Tajikistan, and then a return there, after the Wakhan expedition, which seemed to confound them. Tajikistan, although landlocked, is also something of a dead end, being surrounded either by the Oxus barrier to the south, or by the Tien Shan and Pamir to the south and east, so the concept of double entry visas was not well understood. But when we failed in London and Washington, we found a resourceful official in the Tajik Embassy in Brussels, who decided he could be creative, and agreed.

When Dillon arrived he stayed with a friend in Epsom, and I went, with some trepidation, to meet him there. I drove past the sodden sweep of Epsom race courses's Tattenham Corner, dreary and empty of horses on a wintry wet June day, into a warren of streets behind and found him. Soon we were exchanging ideas and reminiscences, chatting about characters in the history of Asian exploration, and I felt at ease; there was no doubt that we shared objectives and ambitions, and he had the most valuable asset of all, he laughed a lot.

There are only two legal ways to reach the Wakhan Corridor: one is via Kabul and a three day journey north to Ishkashem, the gateway town at the western end of the Wakhan; or via either Dushanbe in Tajikistan, or Bishkek in Kyrghizia and then travel south, to the international frontier at Ishkashem, where the Oxus emerges from the Wakhan and begins its progress up through the mountains around the northern provinces of Afghanistan.

It was certainly physically possible to enter Wakhan via one of the passes from Pakistan, such as Baroghil, Irshad, or Kilik. However, given the volatile security situation in this region, permission for such entry would never be granted, by either the Afghan or Pakistani authorities. The motives of any foreigners attempting a mountain crossing illegally here would be interpreted as hostile.

We decided to take the Tajik route as this gave us the best chance of reaching all possible sources of the river, given that we would start with the relatively simple access to the first of them, Lake Syr Kul.

The plan was to travel south from Bishkek, Kyrghizia to the Tajik border south of Osh and due south to Murghab, then to Syr Kul on the Afghanistan border and follow the Panj River branch of the Oxus to Ishkashem, where we would enter Afghanistan. We would then turn back up the river on the Afghan side until we reached Qala Panj, and east into the Wakhan Corridor itself, to Sarhad/Boroghil, where the route starts across the Wakhan Massif into the high Pamir on the other side. All the other sources would be found in the High Pamir on the other side of the Massif.

We would be would be travelling on paved, or semi-paved roads through Kyrghizia, and at least as far as Murghab, then off road, apart from the approach to Ishkashem on the Tajik side. Once in Afghanistan we would be able to use vehicles as far as Sarhad; thereafter it would be on foot across the Wakhan Massif, and the Pamir to the east. The overall journey within the Wakhan would be about 750 kilometres, of which nearly half would be on foot and mostly at over 13,000 feet.

Timing was critical. Previous travellers here had many different views on the accessibility of the various routes and passes. Certainly we should be able to cross the river where we needed to, at Ishkashem, and possibly further upstream at Langar. Thereafter there should be fording points in the Wakhan valley. But it was hard to tell how far the water in the river would have fallen following the spring melt. We could be there too early, or too late, and be overtaken by winter in the Pamir.

At Bishkek we met our guide for the Pamir mountain section, a tall rugged Tajik, called Ergash Fayzellobekov, and his driver, neither of whom had ever visited Kyrghizia before. The Aeroflot in-flight magazine had mentioned a grand new Hyatt hotel, so we directed Ergash towards Bishkek, and maybe a good breakfast. Nothing looked less likely as we entered the cool, wide, scruffy streets of the town, but we didn't care, the thrill of Central Asia had taken hold of us; the great Tien Shan range could be seen to the east, and not far over the other side was the teeming cosmopolitan market city of Kashgar, a Turkic city in Chinese Xingiang province.

However we did find the hotel, it was open, and we had a breakfast which was well worth the wait: omelettes flavoured with small scarlet berries, and basins of almond flavoured coffee.

It seems to be one of those general rules of travel that somehow, somewhere you always run into the people that you need. Thus the only other guests for breakfast were two executives from the Aga Khan Foundation (AKF) who knew our driver; he was actually one of their part-time employees. One of the two knew as much about the Wakhan as anyone I had met. They had heard of our plans and wanted to offer their support. AKF is the only outside organisation working in the area, and their influence is more useful than any Government organisation.

We left Bishkek to the South East, after a number of trial runs down the wrong roads as the wide boulevards do not bother with street signs.

Soon it was hot, and we were climbing into the mountains. We crossed two passes of around 8,000-9,000 feet, one ending in a long tunnel, which dropped down to the marvellously beautiful Kara Suu Lake, an aquamarine bath surrounded by mountains swathed in billiard-table green.

That night we reached Osh, the second city of Kyrghizia. A lone traveller would have been hard pressed to find hotel rooms, as the city doesn't seem to cater for visitors. Ours were located in an unmarked building above a bank. The hostess was happy and friendly, and charged us about ten dollars each. There was an old man outside our rooms, selling the traditional Kirghiz drink of salty milk; he spoke excellent English, but wouldn't explain when or where he had learned it, strange in a country where for more than fifty years only Russian would have been a useful second language.

We had a street-side dinner of mutton, chicken and beer, tapped from a barrel, alongside some noisy military men. Many Kirghiz are of Mongol descent and their flat faces do not suit the wide Russian style military caps.

It was a tight squash to fit five people in the 4x4, and one person had to sit in the middle, at the back with no seatbelt, in a very uncomfortable position for long stretches over rough tracks. Unfortunately for Ergash, since we were his customers, he was the one who had to perch there for the whole journey. Hossein was a superlative driver though, and seemed to know, or anticipate every pothole, rock fall, and hidden crevice in the Pamir before they were visible to the rest of us.

We passed through more sweepingly soft green valleys, home to Kirghiz nomads' low white tents or yurts. They are made of canvas or felt, wound around wooden batons, with either a hole in the roof or a tin chimney for smoke to escape. They are divided into living and kitchen areas, and also have defined male and female sections, even though the lines of demarcation seem invisible to outsiders. The yurts are moved during the seasons, in caravans, as the pastures change. They're dismantled, loaded onto yaks or mules and transported to the next, greener pastures. However here the occasional yurt has a car parked alongside, even though there is only one road in the area.

It was wet and cold as we rose into the Alai Mountains and approached the Tajik frontier. At the border post, simply a concrete hut and shelter, it was snowing. We were greeted by some six or seven variously-dressed officials, who seemed to be bored with life and took all our papers into the hut for an extended consultation. Eventually they returned and asked us to stand in a line. One of them held out the Irish passport and called for 'Sir Kitcheen'. Anthony stepped forward and was greeted with the words that after several repetitions we understood to be 'Irish Republican Army; Hooray'. Now Anthony comes from one of the old Anglo-Irish Protestant families, but he immediately held out his hand and repeated the 'Hooray'. We had presents for them; fat round breads and onions, not as bribes, simply a neighbourly gesture to officials who would surely prefer to be elsewhere.

The Tajik frontier, a few miles further on, consists of a pair of cylindrical, blue corrugated, iron huts. More bread passed hands, and a bit of hugging and clasping between the Tajiks. I would have liked a bit of hugging too as it was then very cold.

19th century engraving of Ovis Poli

CHAPTER SIX

Pilgrims and Dragons

Passing fold after fold of ever higher ranges it was clear how the Pamir had been for the 19th-century geographers the other dark, impenetrable heart, alongside Central Africa. Marco Polo was the first recorded Western traveller to Pamir. But Polo's 'Travels' is no more helpful or communicative about routes, inhabitants, or even means of survival in Pamir, than it is for most other parts of the journey. He might have used the Wakhan to go through the Pamir or travelled further north or possibly he was never there at all.

Even as late as the early 19th century the only other available reports were those the Portuguese Jesuit, Benjamin Goez, and some medieval period Chinese Buddhist pilgrims. None had made any progress towards establishing where the Oxus, or the other rivers of Turkestan rose. They did manage to create, for the Victorian British and Tsarist Russian explorers, a sense of mystery and adventure, so that the first serious attempts to reach the Pamir in the mid 19th century were much anticipated and discussed.

What Curzon referred to as the '…Oxus, that great parent stream of humanity' was effectively unexplored above its most southerly point at Ishkashem. There was myth, folklore and speculation but little else. In

Central Asia the mountains had long been worshipped as gods themselves or, as animist theologies developed, the home, or conduit for the gods. 'The Roof of the World' was almost completely unknown. For the Hindus the Pamir was the unknown Aryan Paradise, whence water flowed via the four great rivers of Asia; Ganges, Oxus, Indus and Sita (possibly the Tsangpo/Brahmaputra, which they mistakenly thought to rise in the Roof of the World region).

Both Persian and Zoroastrian beliefs also incorporate the Pamir and the Oxus in their histories. The Persian *Vendidad*, which describes the fifteen origins of the Persian race, includes amongst them the land of the Seven Rivers, which was their name for the middle and upper Oxus.. The Zoroastrian traditions looked to the Pamirs for their Gods. Zoroaster was held to have resided in Balkh at the western end of the Afghan Oxus and the fires started by the thunderbolts of the Gods were to the east in the mountains.

For the Buddhists too, the Pamir was the revered and unknown source of water and mystery. Their traditions held that rivers flow from a central lake in the Pamir. This is reflected in the Chinese Buddhist writings, in which the four rivers are sourced together from Dragon Lake in the centre of a plateau known as the Sumeru of the Gods.

In the 7th century Chinese Buddhist converts sought the ultimate spiritual journey to the foundation sites of their new faith and travelled across Turkestan and the mountains to what is now Pakistan. Most celebrated amongst these was Hwen-Tsuang. When he returned in AD 644 he seems to have taken a trans-Pamir route and held this to be the Sumeru or land of the Gods. *'In the middle of the high valley is the Dragon Lake. The water is pure and clear as a mirror; it cannot be fathomed. It is bright blue and the taste of the water is sweet and soft. In the water hide kauki fish, turtles, dragons and crocodiles. On the east of the lake is a great stream. Passing over a mountain to the south of the valley, we find the country of Po-lo-lo; here is found much gold and silver. Along the route there are no men or villages. Ascending the mountains… we encounter nothing but ice, snow and precipices'.*

Most of the historical commentary was speculation because the writers had no idea what was within and beyond the Pamir. So on the principle of 'what they do not know, they deify' it was considered to be the abode of Gods, and Paradise, in the same way as Mesopotamia was viewed as the earthly paradise for the Semitic Jews.

The search for the Dragon Lake had been registered in the public mind as one of the great grails of 19th-century travel.

رود خانه السوس

CHAPTER SEVEN

Syr Kul – The First Source

Our first objective was to find Lake Syr Kul, where in 1838 a young British Naval Lieutenant, John Wood, was the first man of the modern era to stand in the Pamir and confidently claim to have found both Dragon Lake and the source of the Oxus.

An hour or so after the Tajik border-post, we reached the fifteen thousand feet Kizil Art pass. Here we saw the only car that we were to see in all day, other than at the small town of Murghab, where the road from China crosses the river. It was another Aga Khan Foundation vehicle, so the driver was well known to ours. They stopped to talk, and clearly had a newspaper full of news to discuss between them.

Down from the pass, the small road is dead straight for tens of kilometres until Kara Kul becomes visible in the distance. I had been looking forward to seeing this high, semi-salt lake, as my younger daughter is called Kara, and was keen to see pictures of 'her lake'. Kara is Kirghiz for black; Kul is lake. Kara shares her name with many features of central Asia such as Karakorum (Black mountains in Kirghiz).

It was hard to see the scale of the lake from the shore, as the far side was lost in mist. There was no sun, and the lake was a grey sheen, very different from the description given by the normally modest St George Littledale in 1890: "Kara Kul was, from the top of the mountains, the most beautiful sight we had seen, the bluest of blues, and surrounded by snowy mountains".

Kara Kul was the first of several high lakes that we were to visit, none of which feature on any list of the world's highest lakes, even though they are all higher than Titicaca in Bolivia, which has long claimed the title of highest navigable lake.

This was already Pamir country… long, bath-shaped valleys with little vegetation and no habitation. It was some hours before we saw the first local people that we had seen in Tajikistan. There was an extended family of nomads living in a camp about half a kilometre from the road, though only the women were present, diminutive grandmothers with walnut wrinkled faces and a flock of children. They rushed to meet us, a stream of primary colours across the russet earth. Our offerings of trinkets and toffees were smilingly but shyly welcomed. Another hour or two later, with cold rain now falling we passed the surprising sight of a lone Tajik cyclist.

We were heading for Murghab; the name means 'river of birds' in Farsi. We came into the town as dusk was falling. I had an odd feeling that I recognised this unlikely little town built at 13,500 ft in the Pamirs. It is known for only two things; it is the night stop for trucks from China, taking what they fondly call the Pamir Highway over to Khorog, the administrative capital of the Gorno Badakshan province of Tajikistan. It was also the Russian base in the latter part of the 19th century, whilst their emissary officers did the Tsars' work in laying claim to and exploring the area at the time of the Great Game.

If I had been there before, there could only be one explanation. This was the unnamed place I had landed seventeen years earlier when I had 'hijacked' the flight from Khorog for twenty dollars. Ergash initially doubted this but asked around and found out that there had indeed been flights there during the Soviet occupation, although the airstrip was now unused.

There is little to commend Murghab to the traveller; it is a collection of dull stone shacks, with opaque windows, in rows around the road. It has no centre, and only one building with lights. Ergash planned for us to stay at a hostel that he knew, but this was barred and shuttered. The lit building was a truckers' rest house, but he seemed keen that we should not stay there, so he went in search of the key to an office he knew.

For a while we stayed in the vehicle, and waited. It was raining very hard, and Murghab is not made for rain, it normally gets no more than three inches a year, but an inch had fallen already that night. It was also clear that I had made a mistake by coming so far that day. We had climbed over 11,000 feet, much further than we should have done if we were to avoid altitude sickness.

Dinner was in an almost flooded dive nearby. Rainwater was washing over the muddied threshold. It was a restaurant with three separated booths, decorated with old travel posters from Russia. There was a peculiarly unwelcoming old man, with a handshake like stone, who seemed to be doing no more than guarding an empty room with red walls, and a red floor. A group of young soldiers were the only other diners. They were in demob happy mood, enjoying a moment of what was an obvious luxury for them. They had a bottle of vodka, and soon we had our own, the last alcohol we'd see for many days.

I began to develop the first signs of altitude sickness: bad headaches, nausea, and a general feeling of unease. I could not even look at the food we were served, and began wondering, not for the last time, what had induced me to initiate this venture. I suspect that I was unpleasantly grumpy with these ill effects.

The man with the key to the office was found. There were some beds, but no lights. All five of us complained of the other's snoring, and Dillon, in frustration had to tear an old clock off the wall, as it announced every quarter-hour with a whirring croak. The loo was a hundred yards away in another compound. It was much more of a loo than most we would find on our journey; a wood shack over a hole, which was a little too small for the purpose. One would lie in bed wondering whether it was worth the effort to go, before making the decision to dash there through the pouring rain. Dillon had used the one in the restaurant earlier, from which he returned burdened with unpleasant tales, which we refused to let him tell.

Murghab is the gateway to the Pamir, which is a mountain range quite as unusual as its river. It is the world's only range defined more by what is between the peaks than by the peaks themselves. The mountain profiles were created in the usual way by retreating glaciers, which deposited rubble and silt, torn from the cliffs and walls. This would normally, in the geological sense, be scoured and washed away by newly formed rivers. In the Pamir, however, where there is little precipitation, this did not happen, so instead of acute V-shaped valleys emerging between the peaks, as they did in the Alps, Andes and Himalaya, there remain wide upland plains, called Pamirs. Many of these are no more than 2,000-3,000 feet below the surrounding summit ridges. The Pamirs are green and yellow with vegetation in summer, an unlikely sight for those who have seen only the barren uplands of Karakorum, or the nearby Hindu Kush. The plains are thirteen to fourteen thousand feet, roughly level with the summit of Mont Blanc, for example, and well above most of the huge Tibetan plateau to the east.

There are eight major Pamirs. Six are which are in the Gorno-Badakshan region of Tajikistan. One, the Little Pamir is in the Wakhan Corridor of Afghanistan. One, the Tagdumbash Pamir, is mainly in China's Xinjiang Province; it extends north from below the Khunjerab Pass in Pakistan to Tashkurgan then past to the magnificent mountain duo of Kongur and Mustagh Ata. These are fraternal twin mountains, standing almost alone. Both are about twenty five thousand feet and belong to that very rare group amongst huge mountains that can be seen from plateau to peak, rather than just as another spike in a range. Although appearing to be alone, they abut the Kun Lun, the last of the five great ranges that have bulldozed each other together over millenia to create the Pamir Knot. The great Himalaya chain presses in from the east; the younger sharper Karakorum, with almost half of the world's 8,000 metre peaks at its centre, from the south; the long sweep of the Hindu Kush (the meaningful English translation is Hindu Killer), which is the natural frontier of the sub-continent; and the Pamirs themselves. Their juncture is a sky high tangle, a

Above: Nomad sisters north of Murghab
Below: John Wood's Lake Syr Kul

Above: Saifal from Sarhad
Below: Wakhi girl near Ishkashem

Above: Oxus in the Wakhan Massif
Below: The only bridge in the Wakhan Massif

Above: Sakhi
Below: On the trail east of Sarhad

Above: Pack horse falls into the river
Below: Little Pamir close to Lake Chakmaktin

Above: Nomad family in the Little Pamir
Below: Wakhan Oxus towards exit from the High Pamir

Above: A little oasis of plenty in the Lower Wakhan
Below left: Kirghiz young woman on the Little Pamir
Below right: Kirghiz boy in the family yurt

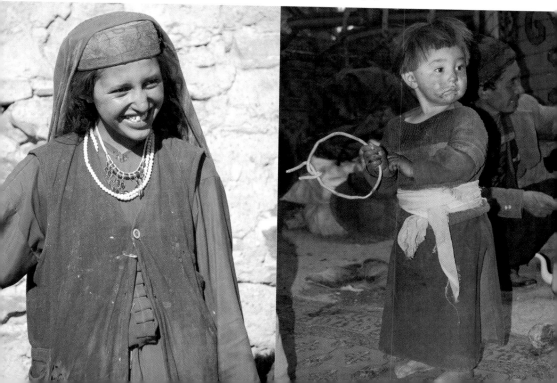

Above: Family on the move
Below: Cooking lessons in the yurt

forbidding geological fist, that together with the Pamirs themselves, is called the Roof of the World.

To the north is the Tien Shan range, which provides the geographical boundary between Chinese and Russian Turkestan. To its west is Kyrghizia and to its east the Taklamakan desert and Tibet. Tien Shan is not quite part of the Pamir Knot but together they create the geographical feature that has helped to mould the recent history of Central Asia. They make the north western access to India very difficult. India is guarded to the north by the ribbon massif of the Himalaya, and beyond by the endless permafrost plateau of Tibet that would sap the resources of any potential invader, however well supplied. West of the Himalaya, the jumbled mass of the Pamir Knot likewise would absorb and dissipate any force that tried to reach the subcontinent. None have ever tried. The only realistic route to India has therefore always been in a wide sweep round to the west, which means crossing the Oxus somewhere, traversing what is now Afghanistan and then the easier ranges of the Hindu Kush, such as through the Khyber Pass.

The route to Wood's Syr Kul first follows the established road east to Ishkashem and Khorog. After an hour or so we turned south and ascended onto the first Pamir. There is no established track, and none is necessary. A defile in the hills opens into a flat plain, two or three kilometres wide, and more than ten in length. From a distance it seemed to be covered in thick, lime green grass; close up it was sparse, but tall and waving in a gentle breeze. We were on top of thousands of feet of glacial moraine, deposited over centuries and filling up the valley. It was a gentle, welcoming, and tangibly peaceful landscape. We climbed an escarpment into the next Pamir, and descend to a lake, unmarked on the map, but as beautiful and surprising to us as Kara Kul had been to the early European explorers, more than a hundred years ago. All around were families of marmots, and the lake, set in a background of yellow summer flowers, was temporary home to a nation of geese. Here travel was like that in the Sahara Desert where the landscape seems to change with the light, and the angle of ascent and distances are hard to estimate. We could choose our route randomly across the empty, bright Pamir, which was taking us south towards Lake Syr Kul.

A few black dots marked the end of the valley. Eventually these dots became three huts, and a stockade for animals corralled by fencing which was built entirely out of yak dung. There were five small children to welcome us. We gave them sunglasses as presents, and they all looked much brighter and happier in their new shades, as they grinned at us, and laughed at each other. These were not just frivolous gifts however, but were valuable assets at these altitudes, where eye problems are widespread.

We left the stockade on a track to the west, but after a while Anthony expressed a concern that had been niggling us all; we seemed to be going too far west. We were indeed on the wrong cross valley, and had to backtrack for some time. To the south we could see a mountain range which would be the Tajik Afghan frontier mountains, dividing the Big from the Little Pamir.

Syr Kul lies at about fourteen thousand feet on the Big Pamir, and by all accounts drains westwards. All the streams were still travelling eastwards, so we were not yet at the watershed. The going was difficult because the ground, which was mainly tussocks of tough grasses on a grey white earth was hard, but often gave way to damp or water filled troughs. Even the great driver, Hossein, had to be very careful.

I was still feeling thoroughly out of condition from the altitude, when we came to a group of three yurts, housing a group of Kirghiz nomads. It was a small family, but probably part of larger group. They were very rich, in Kirghiz terms, as they had many head of goat and yak. Of course they invited us in to eat, it being natural and expected for the nomad to look after and feed travellers. Scents of old leather and the dung fire blended with yak butter inside the yurt…the same welcoming smell that is the signature for the whole Tibetan plateau, not so far away to the east.

This became our first introduction to the milk products that dominate the diet of this high region; it included three different yogurts, and golden double yak cream, that would be the envy of any three star Michelin chef, as well as every creamery in Padstow. Our hosts watched us eat, but did not participate. The men sat with us on multi-coloured sparkling cushions, and offered sheepskin blankets for our legs. The women and children huddled around the fire, partly screened from view.

The going was difficult in the afternoon, as there were small rivers running towards Syr Kul, as soon as we passed the watershed. It took many attempts to find crossing points. Crest after shallow crest was passed, but we found no lake. When it did slowly emerge from its hiding, in a high depression, it was sparkling blue and silver, reflecting the summer browns, and snow peaks of the Wakhan range that mark the Corridor, and Afghanistan. We bounced and bumped around its northern shore for nearly an hour before finding its dwindling, pointed end.

We almost missed the exit point, which was hidden among rushes, a ten metre overflow, knee deep, and shot with peaty tussocks. This was the Panj Oxus. John Wood must have looked at this outlet in 1838 and wondered how something so simple as a fortuitous drainage channel, could become, further on, of such political significance.

For the second time I was able to stand and watch my river. Here it was, new born, lemon clean, and starting its long journey east and then north. Within a few yards of its birth it was already strong with the 'bright speed of its high mountain cradle in the Pamere'.

Sir Alexander ('Bokhara') Burnes 1805–1841

CHAPTER EIGHT

John Wood and the Dragon Lake

Wood may have been the first modern Westerner to find Syr Kul, but others had been scrapping at the edge of the Pamir before he did.

The mid 19th century was an age when travellers and explorers were trophy hunters. They sought firsts like mountaineers, not only for their own glory, but for the political ends of their countries. The British in particular considered the area to be their own, and treated each new attainment as a matter of national pride and achievement. Some of them were also the MI5 of their generation. They answered their countries' need to get information and understanding of unknown territories.

The mystery of the source of the Oxus was publicized by 'Bokhara' Burnes. Alexander (later Colonel Sir Alexander) Burnes was an explorer in search of fame and glory. Aged 27 he and Dr James Gerard, both travelling under the aegis of the Honourable East India Company, became the first Europeans to reach Bokhara. Disguised as Afghans they travelled across the Oxus in north west Afghanistan. They were light in terms of attendants but in other respects had all the accoutrements of the traditional spy; many different passports sewn into their clothing, strings of gold ducats hidden in shoes and waistbands. Burnes returned from his trans-Oxus adventure in 1832, and went as fast as possible to London, where he announced his success to the Board of the Company, and to the Royal Geographical Society. He was treated like a modern day sports hero, but with an added political dimension. Burnes's book *Travels into Bokhara* (1834) became a best seller as an adventure story that intrigued the reading public, and hinted at lands and people as yet unknown. Burnes had never been anywhere near the Roof of the World, so much of his information was hearsay. His descriptions of the Pamirs and Transoxiana, for example, were based entirely on information gleaned from merchants that he met in Kunduz (North Afghanistan). However his public neither knew nor cared and 'Bokhara Burnes' was an immediate celebrity, who achieved a status to which other travellers aspired.

He titillated the early Victorians with his stories of licentious Yarkand, where the women had many temporary husbands. He enthused and inspired all but one of the travellers that followed him with speculation about the Dragon Lake and the source of the Oxus in the Pamirs.

The one exception to this was the extraordinary figure of Alexander Houghton Gardiner, most of whose exceptional journeys were already completed before Burnes had left school. Gardiner needed no more catalyst than his own energy, and sometimes the urgent need to leave problems behind. He was the one traveller that was to publicly claim that he had already reached the source of the Oxus before Lieutenant Wood. In fact he claimed to have found nineteen different sources, but he never provided any geographical detail to enable his contemporaries to identify even one of them.

He was a loner, a soldier of fortune, explorer and maybe fantacist and later a fictional anti-hero in George MacDonald Fraser's *Flashman and the Mountain of Light*. For nearly 50 years, often sporting his red Cameron Lochiel tartan he bestrode Central Asia and North India, as adventurer and storyteller.

Gardiner had left Central Asia and was in Lahore as commander enforcer in the service of Ranjit Singh, Maharajah of Punjab, by the time that Lieutenant Wood set out for the Pamir in 1838 and for sure Wood had no knowledge of Gardiner's as yet unpublished memoirs. Whether or not Gardiner did find the sources of the Oxus, he was the most colourful figure in all of Central Asian exploration and despite his many contemporary detractors deserves his place in its history. The remarkable life story of Gardiner and his various claims about his travels in Central Asia are considered in the Appendix I.

In their very different ways Gardiner and, later, Curzon both chose to be adventurers. Wood became one by default. He was a naval engineer, who was sent in 1837, as part of an expedition on its way to Kabul to investigate the navigability of the Lower Indus, for trade and military purposes. He was not very impressed with his assignment, as it hardly required his skills; anyone with a lead, long stick or other measuring device, plus some advice from locals on seasonal changes could have done the job. His eventual conclusion was that there was no river of even half the water volume in the whole area, which was less suitable for navigation.

Wood's value on the expedition once they reached Afghanistan was nil. Alexander Burnes, now resident in Kabul put him to use exploring a northerly route from Jellalabad to Kabul via the Karkatcha Pass as he was trying to complete a new map of the country. That was until he was recalled, and instructed to accompany a Dr Lord, who was being sent to the apparently barbarous north east.

The reason for Dr Lord's journey was that gifts had been brought to Dost Mohammed, the ruler of Kabul, on behalf of the Uzbek ruler of Kunduz, Murat Ali Beg. Murat brother's Mohammed Beg had developed a bad disease of the eye and Murat Ali Beg thought that the British doctor might be able to help him. Presumably there was no one better or otherwise qualified and so Wood was chosen to accompany this party that would surely gain kudos and influence for the British with the Kunduz tyrant and his brother.

The route to the upper reaches of the Oxus and Turkestan necessarily required the party to take one of the passes across the Hindu Kush. They chose to go via the Parwan Pass, and eventually the Salang Pass. After encounters with bandits and the death of several retainers of a fellow

Afghan traveller, they were forced to turn back. Some 140 years later the Russian invaders encountered similar problems getting between Kabul and their northern supply routes, and therefore built the Salang Tunnel in the 1980s, which has become a notorious feature of the local battles for power in Afghanistan.

They returned to Kabul and took the easier route via Bamian instead. They reached Kunduz and the powerbase of Murad Beg on 4th December, about one month after setting out from Kabul. The town was no more than a few hundred mud huts, and a rudimentary fortress with a moat, which could be flooded as a defensive measure, and housed the citadel of Beg himself.

Wood compares Murad Beg to Ranjit Singh (of Lahore) as a man who ruled through mental strength. Beg had total authority in his domain. "There is not a man in his dominions, possess what authority he may, but he must yield it up at the nod of the Mir. Their services are placed at all times at his disposal". He describes Beg as "but the head of an organised banditti, a nation of plunderers, whom however none of the neighbouring states can exterminate". Beg seemed to be capable of bringing together fifteen thousand armed horsemen in a short time if needed.

Wood could have been describing modern Afghan leaders from the same areas such as Gulbuddin Hekmatyr, the scourge of the Soviets and later the Americans, Abdul Rashid Dostum or Ahmed Shah Massoud, his equivalents in the 1980s, '90s and following the US invasion of 2003. Not much changes in the bellicose politics of Afghanistan.

After a week in Kunduz it was clear that there was little that Dr Lord could do to restore the sight of Mohammed Beg's poor eye, but he was able to use what skill he had, to help preserve the less damaged one. Wood did not want to overwinter there. He wrote: "The great object of my thoughts by day, and my dreams by night, had for some time been the discovery of the source of the River Oxus …and on December 10th Murad Beg gave me his permission to trace the course of the Jihun (Uzbek name for Oxus)".

Between Kunduz and Fayzabad, Wood travelled along the banks of the Kokcha River. He then did something that came naturally to most other 19th century travellers in the Pamir, but seems a little out of character for

Wood; he went partridge shooting, for sport, along the river. Despite claiming that the birds all fly down the river rather than over the guns, they bagged five hundred partridge. "It was extremely cold but we were well clad, and a brisk canter through the snow on such a day gives a new impulse to the spirit, a new value to existence".

He was in Badakshan, principally a Tajik and Shia area, naturally opposed to the Uzbeks, and often at war with them. He was also deep in the Oxus valley, further than any of the Tartar invaders, Genghiz Khan or Tamerlane had reached. By 4th February they had reached Jerm, the largest place in Badakshan at the time, with some fifty houses. From there they crossed the Ishkashem Pass, with the mountains of Chitral in the Hindu Kush to the south, and emerged onto the narrow Ishkashem plain and the Oxus valley. They met a lone traveller wrapped in the skin of a horse. He was the only one of a party of Badakshanis caught up the river by the snows who had escaped; he had done so by sacrificing his horse for food and clothing. At Ishkashem they crossed the Oxus, which seemed to him to be thirty five metres wide when frozen, but is likely to have been somewhat wider. They were truly in the Wakhan now.

It was a cold and lonely journey of forty miles up the uninhabited Oxus valley to the Tajik village of Kundut. The only living thing encountered was one hare. Kundut had fifteen houses and a big fire where they were housed and welcomed. Thereafter the very few inhabitants were Kirghiz and their stock were yak, which Wood describes as no more than three and a half feet high with the belly almost touching the ground, like a large Newfoundland dog. And he commented: "If unable to praise the men for their good looks, I may without flattery pronounce the young women pretty".

The houses were kirgah (yurt) with open domes for smoke and ventilation. As today each kirgah could be readily dismantled and then carried by no more than three yaks to the next camp. One takes the skeleton, consisting of side wall trellising and seventy or more roofing stakes, and looks like a big ungainly hedgehog; one takes the felts and wrappings, the third the furniture and equipment.

Wood had brought snuff as offerings for the Tajik and Kirghiz.

Nothing could have been more popular, except that he did not have enough. Not content with a more delicate Victorian style pinch for each nostril the Kirghiz simply took all that was offered and ate it.

Twenty five miles or so up the valley they reached Langar/Qala Panj and what was the critical moment of the whole journey, even though Wood was not aware of it at the time. At Langar the river divides: one branch goes northeast into the Pamirs (the Panj) and one southeast into the Wakhan. Wood had to decide which was the senior branch to follow upstream. He did not know that some fifty plus years later Curzon would re-examine the reasons for this decision in great detail as part of his attempt to establish his, Curzon's, claim to have found the real source of the river.

The decision that John Wood made was to follow the northern branch of the river, and it was to influence the course of Oxus exploration for most of the next sixty years. He made the decision based on his own observations of the relative size of the two rivers, and detailed questioning of the local Wakhanis. The latter must have been the primary determinant, as the two rivers at Qala are different; the Panj is narrower, faster and deeper than the Wakhan/ Sarhad, which has already spread wide across the Wakhan valley. It is likely that Wood also relied on relative temperatures of the two rivers and concluded that the Panj, as the colder river was likely to be sourced higher in the Pamirs.

Having made the decision, Wood and his party set off towards what they believed would be the Roof of the World, in the High Pamir. It was getting very cold indeed. On the second night the mercury in the thermometers disappeared into the bulb, indicative of a temperature well below six degrees Fahrenheit. They created a fire as best they could and slept with their feet as close to it as possible.

At over thirteen thousand feet the altitude was beginning to hamper their progress and deplete their effectiveness. The cold did have the advantage that they were able for some time to travel on the frozen river itself, but it was not just snow on top of an even sheet of ice; the ice was striated with seracs and they had to force a path through the imperfectly frozen surface. The Kirghiz horsemen found what seemed to be an unlikely camp place but they knew what they were doing and had soon uncovered mounds of yak and camel dung to use as fuel for the night.

The route was leading higher all the time. By the end of the next day and more than a thousand feet higher, feet and there was nascent mutiny in the camp as even the Kirghiz, who had been following a known track, now wanted to turn back. Every step had to be hacked through the snow. Horse after horse had to be sent into the van to plough out a path for the rest, and within minutes lay panting in the rarified air. As they approached what seemed to be a flatter plain that could host the source, the ice became brittle on the river, and they had to revert to the banks. This was signalled by the loss of a mule through the ice, which eventually reappeared and somehow survived through the heroic ministrations of its owner.

"After quitting the river, we travelled for about an hour along its banks and then ascended a low hill, which apparently bounded the valley to the eastward; on surmounting this, at five o'clock on the afternoon of 19th February we stood upon the Bam-i-Duniah, or Roof of the World, while before us stretched a frozen sheet of water, from whose western end issued the infant river Oxus". This was Lake Sarikol or Syr Kul as it now is called (marked A on the map on pages 8/9). It was surrounded by the Pamir and Wakhan mountains, but not at all dominated by them. Wood's report was the first modern description of any part of the Pamir. He was convinced, not unreasonably, that he had found both the source and the fabled Dragon Lake.

This was the first of five times in the next hundred and seventy years that one or more travellers would stand over a Pamir stream and confidently claim to have found the true source of the great river Oxus. However for a least the next 50 years following the publication of his reports, Wood was recognised as the explorer who at last had done so.

To some degree he must have been disappointed, although he gives no indication of this. Syr Kul is big, very big, for a lake at this altitude, but it is also very shallow. There were few signs that it could have been the home for the wild or unusual beasts that the medieval stories had claimed. Nor could it have been the source of rivers, or even streams travelling west towards China or eventually India. The only exit was the westward-flowing Oxus.

CHAPTER NINE

A Policeman, A Doctor and Two Innkeepers

Wood returned as fast as he could down the frozen river, and we took the same route following the Afghan frontier but in much pleasanter conditions. It was a further six hours to Langar, where we would stay for the night, the last two of which were on reasonably well-established roadways beside the river, sometimes very high above the river and sometimes close alongside. There seemed to be more livestock, such as camel, yak and goat on the Afghan side than the Tajik side but there were no established roads or tracks that we could see. The two great Pamir Peaks, Engels and Karl Marx, dominated the western horizon, substantially higher than anything else, until the much sharper Hindu Kush peaks appeared to the South.

These were the Wakhan frontier with Pakistan. We were funnelled by the two ranges down the Oxus gorge. The river was becoming more aggressive and fierce as it gathered size, and prepared to merge into the Wakhan Oxus, at Langar, the location of Wood's decision between steams to follow, and where the valley flattens fast, and opens into a morass of intertwined streams from both directions.

Wood was right; there is no way to assess which was the real parent stream at that point. He could do little else than accept the opinions of his guides and the locals of Langar, and so he opted for the northern branch. We reached the confluence in the evening. There was a guest house with two rooms, in one of which a very ill person, maybe another traveller, was moaning on a bed, so we all took the other. Behind the building was an irrigation stream that passed for a washroom.

Langar is an oasis with trees, mainly high altitude poplars, evidence that we had descended several thousand feet during the day. They obscured a good view across the confluence of the rivers, but in the twilight one could make out the steeply rising mountainsides on the other side, that created the tunnel valley which would take us into the Wakhan itself. I should have been eager with anticipation. Instead I felt depressed, even homesick. I wandered through the village trying to find a way to the river, so as to get a better view of the valley, and was consumed not by excitement, but by the apparent pointlessness of this escapade and a loss of confidence in either our ability to succeed or our purpose.

"No one cares where the real source of the river is, or indeed who, or when, it is or was discovered", I said to myself, miserably. "What is the point of dragging the others up the mountains, with little idea where we are going, or why, when we could all be doing something useful". Even less should anyone care whilst there is a war throughout much of Afghanistan which had again torn this ravishing, but so often ravished country apart. Was I not, still the same vertigo afflicted man who had lied to my six year old daughter that the Eiffel Tower was closed, so as to avoid having to go to the top?

It was probably the unwelcome memories of Shor's description of the journey ahead that I had allowed myself to recall too vividly; maybe it was also the altitude sickness, but I had not felt like that since my early years as a schoolboy, where I had often felt very much alone, despite being in company. I did not tell the others but I ate nothing that night, and must have been bad company.

In the morning I found Dillon sitting on a makeshift chair carefully writing his diary and looking every bit the acclimatized traveller that I was not. It was about six hours on down river to Tajik Ishkashem, which is where Wood crossed the river for the first time, and now the only legal entry point in the north east. We began to see a few more people as we arrived. There was a little tarmac on the route but it was used more for carpet cleaning than traffic, and several times we had to stop for sodden soapy rugs to be pulled off the surface for us to pass.

The Wakhan Corridor forms the easternmost extremity of Afghanistan in the Pamir Mountains. It connects Afghanistan to China in the east and separates Tajikistan in the north from Pakistan in the south. Although notionally part of Afghanistan it is really more of a no-man's-land, a buffer between the subcontinent and the Russias. It is a high altitude cradle that holds the young Oxus river. The inner areas have always been difficult to access. For much of the 20th century it was also politically inaccessible. It is this mysterious, unknown few hundred square miles high in the mountains that is the focus of this story.

There are three distinct parts to the Wakhan. The western end, where the Corridor flows out into the Afghan province of Badakshan, is the Tajik or Dari speaking area around the access town of Iskashem. The accepted leader of this apparently conservative Sunni community was Sadhar Khan, a mujahadeen commander, with a history of fighting Russians and Taliban. He had become a close lieutenant of Ahmad Shar Massoud 'the Lion of the Panjshir', the most successful of all the mujahadeen commanders fighting the Soviet forces after 1979. Sadhar Khan's power in the area was considered absolute and was fiercely enforced. He was also the man, though at the time I did not know this, who had been two years earlier the lynchpin in the remarkable Greg Mortensen's campaign to build schools in Wakhan villages. His first school for boys, and the almost universally as yet uneducated, girls had been built in Sadhar Khan's home village of Baharak. (see Appendix III: Greg Mortensen and the Stones into Schools programme). He may have secured his power with protection money from opium traders and other smuggling operations; but it was wielded with benevolence and in the interests of his people as he saw them.

The only route east into the Wakhan Corridor itself is up river and into the Wakhi-speaking, Ismaeli community of the river valley, from where would be drawn most of our porters and horsemen for the journey beyond. There are twenty or so villages, on the south, or Afghan, side of the river. On the north, Tajik, side it is too precipitous for anything other than marmots, the high altitude burrowing mammal that looks like a large squirrel. At Qala the Corridor (directly across the river from Langar) turns eastwards into a narrower, deeper valley, to Sarhad, the easternmost permanent habitation in the Wakhan. Qala was the home of the local leader, Shah Ismail Khan, who as an Ismaeli, would have more regard to the patronage of the Aga Khan than any Afghan Government authority, not that there is any evidence of the latter in the Wakhan.

Beyond Sarhad is the Wakhan massif. The crossing of the Wakhan Massif was the major barrier to the journey. It is a sixty-five kilometre stretch of mountain; the route ascends and descends by over 20,000 feet along its length, whilst crossing and recrossing the river that booms through its core. What trail there is clutches the side of steep cliffs of smooth rock and perilously shifting slate. The airless atmosphere at up to 14,000 feet debilitates lowland men and pack animals alike. The prize at the end is the Little Pamir plateau, bounded by China at the far end, Pakistan and the Hindu Kush to the south, and the Great Pamir to the north. The only inhabitants here were reputed to be a few hundred Kirghiz nomads, who make a living from herding yaks and goats. They cross freely between Wakhan and the upper Pamirs with no regard for national boundaries.

One day maybe a road will be constructed through this corridor, which is now known mainly to 19th-century explorers, Kirghiz nomads, and some Russian military conscripts in the 1980s. Until then, the Wakhan remains as it was in the days of Marco Polo, a closed geographical cul-de-sac.

It was a Saturday when we tried to cross into Afghanistan. The border is a bridge over the now quieter Oxus guarded by twenty foot iron gates. It was closed on Saturdays, to all except Tajiks and Afghans, but Ergash was confident that he could have an exception made. Sure enough soon the sixteen foot steel gates to the bridge swung open. Saturday is also market day in no man's land between the frontiers, as a bazaar has traditionally been allowed on this one day of the week. The main attraction for the relatively poor Afghan men was the chance to see women in unveiled dress, and indeed the Tajik women were as brightly dressed as any in Asia.

We were not permitted to visit the market, but we had at least come out of Tajikistan into no man's land. In the melée of market goers at the end of the bridge I was approached by a slightly rotund, well spoken Afghan in shalwar kameez and white baseball cap. His name was Ghulam Sakhi Danishjo, and he was to be our guide. After a cursory few exchanges though, it became disappointingly clear that he had no greater knowledge of the area than we had; he had never even been as far as Ishkashem before. Sakhi introduced us to Nadir, a dark, lean Uzbek, who reminded me of James Coburn in the Magnificent Seven. He was always black dressed and appeared brooding and aloof. He was to to spend many hours contemplating the world on his own, and finding different ways to chastise his perfectly compliant horse. He was the titular leader of the expedition, rather than Sakhi, though he rarely took any decisions; and the one time he did, many days later, he nearly got us into some trouble.

The third team member to meet us there was Sheffi, an Afghan from Faizabad, who had been recruited for us alongside Nadir and Sakhi. Sheffi was older, maybe fifty and a grandfather. He had a brindled beard, hollow cheeks, spiky nose and bright, stone blue eyes. He always wore a light shalwar kameez. He had no Wakhan experience either, but he was, unlike the others, clearly a mountain man, and he knew of the extra demands and risks of mountain travel. He was calm, excellent with his hands, thoughtful and remarkably knowledgeable about the area and its inhabitants. He had an enthusiasm and pride in the untameable grandeur that was his country of Afghanistan. He and many of the others were to humble me with their competence and self-sufficiency, but most of all with their so evident satisfaction with life.

It took several hours of intermittent interview and negotiation to get access to Afghanistan, during which, questions were asked about our various personal biographies including, for instance, detailed questions about my academic qualifications. Several times they apologised, and said that it was all for our own benefit as a Russian had recently been lost in the Wakhan. Anthony's name 'Kitchin' amused them; when Dillon's American passport was handed over, the only comment was a wry: "Ah, here is one of our guest countrymen", one of the few references made by anyone we met on the thousands of American, British and other foreigners then fighting the Taliban, and other antagonists, in their country.

The Afghan Ishkashem is about five kilometres away from its Tajik namesake on the other side of the river, and it is very different. It is more primitive: there are small wooden stores displaying wares on the roadside; the drainage and services are in open troughs at the roadside. The men are uniformly dressed, and no women are visible; school children would timidly survey us from across the road. I was later to find out that these well dressed children were from a school created by the Greg Mortensen's Central Asia Institute.

We went to the office of the Chief of Police, and while Sahki had a lengthy, animated discussion with him, I examined the large scale Wakhan maps on the wall; these were far more detailed than anything else I have seen, other than the Russian military maps. It also gave us all a chance to watch Sakhi in action. He usually wore his grey-white shalwar kameez over a wool jersey, and various forms of headdress, both local, and European, holding in place the ubiquitous Afghan scarf. He had a comfortable, and gentle disposition, and as long as I knew him was at all times a reasonable man. He was a Hazara, a the tribe that is often looked down upon in Afghanistan; however as the only person on the expedition with any English, he was held in some eminence by the others.

It emerged that the argument they were having was about whether or not we wanted an armed escort of police to travel with us into the Wakhan. Sakhi, who was suspicious of the motives of all Afghan police, was against this idea, and seemed to negotiate with confidence and diplomacy. We declined the offer of protection, leaving ourselves the option of changing our minds once we arrived at Sarhad, a pointless qualification, as there would never be a chance of recruiting official support out there.

We soon found that our initial concern about Sakhi's experience was entirely unfounded, and that his overall knowledge of his country, its history and politics was a valuable resource. He was also able to see his way through issues of authority of a country that has always been uncomfortable with statehood and here relies for its stability very much on relationships between village leaders. Sakhi was as new as we were to the Wakhan, but he could have been a veteran for the way he dealt with details of the journey, and the sense of responsibility that he had for the party and the Wakhan itself. Once again I had been lucky in finding good travelling companions.

We stayed at Wafai's guesthouse. Wafai was a father of seven children, six of whom lived with him. He said that he had sent his wife of ten years back to her father as she was an opium addict and had started stealing his possessions. I slept in the big room with Wafai, his six-year-old son and maybe one or two others; it was too dark to see. Several travellers and other guests joined us in the night, so there was quite a party for breakfast.

As soon as we had permission, we left the charming and friendly village of Ishkashem. Our Afghan team had brought with them a Landcruiser, and a white pick-up, as we were carrying baggage for the whole journey. The route took us back up the other side of the Oxus parallel to the journey we had taken the day before. Theoretically the whole two days from Langar, and back up-river again to Qala Panj, on the other side, could have been avoided had we crossed the river at Langar, but this is not a legal entry point, although Afghans do cross here.

Initially there was a rock strewn track; but later it dissolved into the sand and pebble backwash of the river, as it widened in the flatter ground of the beginnings of the narrow part of the Wakhan. We passed six or eight settlements of white, or brown washed stone and plaster houses. By nightfall we arrived, via many diversions for streams and rocks, at the little hamlet of Yorut, to stay in what seemed to be a newly-built guestroom. There was even a drop-loo with a fine view over the valley. This is a gentle and mellow land, lime green in the early summer when the river is often divided into many small channels. There are island oases of pasture in the middle of the river, where stock graze alone well protected from potential predators.

Our room was more of a house. By the door there was a dirt covered area, where people could stand and talk; the rest of the room, about three quarters of the whole space, was a raised platform covered in carpets and rugs. This was our sitting room, dining room and bedroom. It was as cosy and comfortable a way of creating living space as I knew. Still feeling ill, I was able to hide myself under a mass of warm blanketing, and watch proceedings. Anthony was in a garrulous mood and held court, introducing the villagers to the contents of his luggage. Dinner took a very long time, and had clearly been the subject of attention from almost the whole village, since our unexpected arrival. It followed a pattern that was to become familiar. First, the aluminium bowls and water pots were brought out for hand washing; then tarpaulins and cloths were strewn across much of the carpeted area, from which fell mill-wheels of unraised bread; then came the bowls of tasty yoghurts, and lastly, an oily mutton and rice. Most of the male members of the village came to watch us eat, but not to share, despite our repeated offers. There seemed to be a pecking order in which some were allowed to sit with us, while others had to stand and watch. We returned their hospitality with the bangles, medals and sweets that we'd bought from the Indian markets in London's Southall.

By mid morning the next day we had retraced the route up the south bank of the river, turned eastwards into the inner Wakhan.. On our right, the great Hindu Kush stood guard over the approaches to North Pakistan. We were soon stuck in mud whilst trying to drive across a contributary river which was in spate, fed by a magnificent 500ft waterfall. As Hossein worked to try to extract us, I picked my way through the channels towards the centre of the valley.

Langar, where we had stayed two days before was just visible across the wide confluence. On a spit surrounded by the Oxus there was a herd of multi-coloured scrawny goats, tended by a small, young girl, dressed all in red. I watched her though my field glasses and she watched back, wide-eyed at the activity. Back in Ishkashem she would have been veiled, or kept at home, but not here in the Wakhan, where the women were more visible but usually still avoided direct contact.

We stopped further along the river and walked up to a village of about five houses. We were invited to eat with the men of the village, seated shoeless on red brown carpets. The only decoration in the room was one half of the long ballot paper for the 2006 election. Each name on the paper was accompanied by a picture of the candidate. I could see why this bizarre document in Wakhan would have been used as ornament, since the candidates, and the issues they addressed, would have been wholly remote from the Wakhis. Power here in the Wakhan had nothing whatsoever to do with Kabul or the Government of Hamid Karzai. It rested in the hands of local *commandhans,* such as Sadhar Khan at the eastern end of Wakhan and Shah Ismail Khan from Qala. These are the commanders, who guarantee security, mobilise the men against external threats, oversee works such as communications, settle disputes and raise their own taxes.

We recruited a cook from the village for our journey, and lunch started with more of the delicious yoghurt, the kind that make Harrods' finest taste by comparison like liquid cardboard. Then a clucking chicken was brought in for our approval, and quickly despatched leaving a small pool of blood in the doorway. Half an hour later it was a chewy, but crisp main course for seven people.

The village was a neat patchwork of tiny paddy fields, with its own little irrigation system, fed from a higher stream. Each area was served by earthwork channels that could be shut off by a slate or sod dam, to divert water to the next section. This simple agricultural engineering system enabled the water flow to supply the demands of crops as the seasons changed, whilst providing protection against spate conditions. Goats and donkeys roamed freely.

As we left I was surprised to be handed a book by one of our village hosts. It was *The Snow Leopard* by Peter Mathieson, whom I remembered meeting many years before in Pakistan. The driver said it was for a French doctor who lived up the valley; the idea that there might be a French doctor in the Wakhan was an ever bigger surprise.

A few kilometres later, the valley narrowed and the river deepened and increased its speed around a bend, and here it was that we found a house with a satellite dish on the roof, and two windmills working as generators.

It was the house, not of a French doctor, but the very English Dr Alex Duncan, with his wife and four young children, who were just finishing a lesson from their mother, on weights and volumes. Alex, slightly balding, and smiling, in thick brown shalwar kameez, looked like a Franciscan friar, whilst his wife seemed too slight to withstand the Wakhan winters. There was also an 'extreme au pair from Rochdale', as she described herself. Here, I thought, as he served up Nescafe for us, sitting on a log in his compound, was our equivalent of Major Fawcett in Evelyn Waugh's *Handful of Dust*.

Alex was not only the resident Wakhan doctor, but was engaged in an important study on the effects of antibiotics on people who have never been exposed to them before. This is one of the very few places in the world where such experiments can be conducted. We hoped to meet him later as he was planning a journey into the Small Pamir to test Kirghiz nomads for disease and opium addiction, which he assessed as affecting more than twenty five per cent of the population.

The problem had developed from the days after the end of the Soviet occupation. Opium production in the outer Wakhan and transmontane parts of north-east Afghanistan had financed the war against the nascent Taliban control of much of the country. Mujahadeen and other producers were trading the poppy out of the country but had also provided it to local villages in the Wakhan. The results had been calamitous for much of the population. The wealth of many families in livestock and what little other possessions they had been liquidated to finance their drug habits. It was so bad that in 2005, the Kirghiz leader in the inner Wakhan, Adbul Rashid Khan, had even had the revolutionary idea of going to Kabul to elicit the help of the newly elected Hamid Karzai Government for aid to solve the problem. It was a pointless, expensive and unproductive visit; Karzai did not have the power to supply the funds, even if he and his insecure

Government had had the will. So they returned humiliated.

A few hours after leaving Alex and family, the valley had widened out to about three miles, the prospect ahead of us changed: the easy, flat, but boulder strewn riverbed we had been ambling along, ended at a sheer mountain wall; this was the barrier that seals the inner Wakhan. To the south a new valley opened ahead of us, this would be the route to the Boroghil Pass into Pakistan. The Wakhan at this point was only about twenty kilometres wide, and we had reached the end of the road.

The village here was called Sarhad, a name that means border, and this indeed, was what it was; but for us, it was the beginning of a new journey into the little known. The river here, exhausted by its high altitude exertions, dropped out of the mountains and into the wide, open valley below, where it rested a while, before its gentle run south, and its long, hard swing north through the Pamirs.. It was a village spread sparsely across the valley and inhabited by several diverse communities. If there was a centre, it was probably the guest house, built there because of the hot springs over which two bath houses have been built. The keeper of the Guest house was Sarhad's version of Chaucer's innkeeper, who knew everyone and their business. He was keen to describe every previous visitor, and wanted to hug us in repeated greetings with his scrawny and sun-dried frame; it was like kissing a hedgehog. Previous travellers to Sarhad have written of hours of relaxation in the hot waters, which turned out to be disappointingly tepid. Although gin clear they somehow managed to leave one covered in a veneer of grey impermeable dust. However I lay back in the water and reflected that most of the 19th-century explorers in the Wakhan would have also lain where I was, at that moment.

Tomb of Abakh-Hoja in Kashgar.
Kashgar was one of the pivotal destinations for Great Gamers in the late 19th Century

CHAPTER TEN

Sportsmen or Spies

Following Wood's 1838 journey and the publication of his Book *The Pamirs and the Source of the Oxus*, it would be forty years before the Pamir was to be explored again and therefore forty years before Wood's very reasonable conclusions were called into question. The two catalysts for this renewed interest in Pamir travel were political and sporting.

It was the growing strategic importance of what would otherwise be the wild unknown Pamir that led to the renewal of geographical interest. The Tsar's ambitions for Russia, in Central Asia would soon be tested. Both British and Russian Empires had their own reasons for needing to establish, or lay claim to boundaries in the abutment zones of the Pamirs. The most obvious boundary was the Oxus. The 1872-3 Boundary Agreement between Britain and Russia concluded exactly that; the main stream of the Oxus should be the division between the Empires. However it had not occurred to the draftsmen of the treaty that no one yet knew exactly where the main stream was. The British assumed that Wood's source was correct but the Russians may have disagreed. The issue remained to be tested in a confrontation in Wakhan eighteen years after the Treaty was signed.

In the intervening years two other expeditions, with political or military objectives, had cast some doubt on the Wood source. The first was led by an Afghan scout, called 'the Mirza', who was sent by Major Montgomerie, Deputy Superintendant of the Great Trigonometrical Survey to penetrate the Upper Oxus. The Mirza reported that the water from Lake Chakmaktin in the Little Pamir flowed into a stream to the west of the Lake. The French explorer, Guillaume Capus, after consultation with Russian officers, supported the view of the Mirza, that the real source of the river was the stream towards Sarhad from the Little Pamir (marked B on the map p 8/9). These explorers all seemed to agree that this stream was preeminent over the contributary coming down the Wakhan-i-Pamir on its left bank, a decision that would later be challenged by Curzon and others.

Away from politics, Victorian Britain was fascinated with hunting and shooting; bagging game was close to being a sort of rite of passage for well-born sons. The moors, the deer forest, the river, the mountain were the places where gentlemen could prove themselves to themselves, and to others, even if it was just doing brave things to small birds. Most could boast of shooting skills earned in combat with grouse in Yorkshire, and red deer in Scotland, but far more exotic and impressive was to be able to lay claim to chamois in the Alps, markhor or ibex in India, or sand grouse in newly opening East Africa. One fabled animal carried an even more illustrious name; the elusive Marco Polo sheep, or *Ovis Poli*. This was the Central Asian sheep with thick, strong corkscrew horns, first reported in the *Travels* of Marco Polo. It was reputed to be as big as a Highland stag, as wild as an eagle, and as strong as a mountain lion. Its lairs were thought to be only the Pamir and lower Tien Shan. The gloriously named Mountstuart Elphinstone (author of *Kingdom of Kaboul* 1815, the seminal work on Central Asia for much of the 19th century) and others had sent back reports and sketches of Marco Polo sheep, but few had seen them.

Most of the hunters were Indian-based military men, and initially, most of the hunting was in the area between Kashgar, Yarkand, and the north of the Karakorum range. They were junior officers, out for excitement, but also to enhance their reputation in the eyes of their superiors. A knowledge of the frontier lands was an asset that could easily lead to advancement.

In those days, there was a narrow line, at best, to be drawn between sport and scouting, or espionage. The Government was increasingly hungry for information about the lands to the north of the great mountain chains, and to the west of Chinese Turkestan. Several incidents had raised tension. Colonel Durand was sent sent to Hunza to subdue the Kanjutis of that valley, who were much the most active in attacking, and stealing from merchant caravans trying to reach Turkestan. His daring raid had temporarily achieved this objective. But then came news of the murder of Dalgleish, a popular British trader, who worked between Yarkand and Leh. He was shot through the shoulder, and then attacked with a sword by Dad Mohammed, a well known Pathan trader, who had run into trouble with almost everyone with whom he did business, and regularly failed to pay his debts. There were so many witnesses to the unprovoked murder of the unarmed Dalgliesh, that the story was quickly spread. Dad Mohammed was eventually arrested and committed suicide in jail.

Whilst India based sportsmen explorers approached Wakhan from the east and south, others sought to reach it from the north and east. Foremost amongst these were St George Littledale, accompanied by his long suffering wife, then Lord Dunmore and his fellow traveller Colonel Trotter.

St George Littledale started his 1891 report to the RGS as if he sought to be remembered like his fictional contemporary, Mr Pooter in *A Diary of a Nobody*. 'Mrs Littledale and I left England on Thursday 11th April 1980 and reached Odessa on 17th at 11 a.m.' It is one of the few times she enters the story, other than when she is sent forward to parley with what is suspected to be a band of well-armed raiding Kanjutis from Hunza. It seemed to be a matter of: 'send forth the women, as they are less likely to be shot on sight'. Later her great discomfort in crossing a rope bridge is recounted in humiliating detail which ended with her being floated on air-inflated skins over the river below, tied to their baggage. We learn almost nothing of Littledale, or his background from his reports. He made no pretence to be anything other than an amateur sportsman and traveller. Geography and politics completely passed him by; he was there simply to be there. They proceeded around the Black Sea, across the Caspian, and on to the Oxus via Merv (Mary) in modern Turkmenistan, then on to Samarkand and into the Alai Mountains, which we had just crossed in Northern Tajikistan. This was all uncharted territory and they had no useful maps. They eventually found their way to where the lush green lower Alai, scattered with Kirghiz yurts, led into the High Pamir.

The Littledales reached Lake Syr Kul from the same direction as we had, having forded the Murghab River (a contributary of the Oxus, though he would have had no idea of this). There they had problems with his guide and porters; the first escaped in the night, and the latter threatened to desert. They tried to go west down the Panj Oxus to Qala, however, that particular route was impassable with flooding at that time of year. They finally managed to exit the Pamirs via Sarhad, and then through the Boroghil Pass, into what is now the Chitral area of North Pakistan.

On their way back a year later St George Littledale and his wife met in Trebizond, on the Black Sea coast, the next English explorers who were to open new routes in Central Asia, Charles Adolphus Murray, the Earl of Dunmore and Colonel Trotter, both of whom were sportsmen but also geographers. It was Trotter, who would later fight his corner with Curzon, when the latter sought sole credit for finding the source of the river.

Dunmore saw himself as the Victorian hunter whose quarry were the creatures he most admired, the eagle and wild sheep, which he considered the proper competition for the English gun at large. As he wrote:

"Tukta Mohammed, having made his peace with the Chinese, has been released from surveillance under which he had been placed for his suspected Russian sympathies, and came to pay a visit a few days ago. We asked him if he could account for our having had such miserable sport, and he replied that this was the very worst season to come up

here, as the Ovis Poli are always very high on the mountain tops amongst the glaciers .... He said he never heard of any being killed at this time of year and was most astonished when I showed him my five heads, and wondered how I had got them. I explained how I had slept out on the hill night after night and after once seeing them, sticking to them.

"He evidently considered this a great waste of energy and proposed a much easier procedure; 'you come back in the spring, for then they are weak for lack of food and are driven down by the snow into the bottom of the nullahs, where I can chase them with my dogs and you can shoot as many as you please'.

Needless to say, I declined his offer."

Lord Dummore *The Pamirs October 1892*

Sportsmen they may have been, but the big prize was the source of the Oxus. The reports of the Mirza and Capus had dented confidence in Wood's conclusions about Syr Kul. Dunmore and Trotter crossed the Wakhjir Pass into the Wakhan and came down into the Wakhjir valley, which was also great hunting ground for *Ovis Poli*. They were then very close to the Ice Cave that Curzon was to discover three years later. They followed down the Wakhjir-i-Pamir to its confluence with the Little Pamir River and then turned right up the Little Pamir to Lake Chakmaktin, where they established that, contrary to earlier reports there was no westward discharge from the lake. They followed around the lake and there found that instead there was a substantial eastward discharge. This was known but was also thought to flow due east towards Tashkurgan in China. It did not and could not have done; instead they followed it north and realised that it eventually became the Aksu/Mughab river that would join the other major branch of the Oxus at Vomar/Roshan two hundred and fifty kilometres to the west. Their informants claimed the Aksu branch to be the superior at Vomar/Roshan. They were therefore convinced that they had indeed made the defining discovery. They had found the true source of the Oxus (marked C on the map on Pages 8/9) As Trotter was to tell the Fellows of the RGS three years later in front of most of the other advocates of the different theories: "There are red letter days in everyone's life and one for me was when I thought I had discovered the principal source of the Oxus".

Theirs had been a formidable journey in which they suffered every sort of setback and problem, most often from the fearsomely cold weather. The distance they covered, and their undoubted endeavour put them at the forefront of 19th-century Asian travellers. However their achievements are not well known now, partly because Dunmore wrote about his travels with less gusto and colour than a Parliamentary draughtsman. He was no match for the names that would soon follow.

رود خانه آلسوس

CHAPTER ELEVEN

Wild Thyme and Precipices

The story of the journey to the High Pamir is dedicated to Greg Mortensen, a hero in the Wakhan, in north east Afghanistan and in North Pakistan for his schools building programme. He shares my fascination with the Wakhan and in the mystery secreted at its farthest end. Greg has twice tried and not yet reached it, but his influence since our journey most certainly and successfully has, as is described in his book STONES INTO SCHOOLS.

The Littledales, Colonel Trotter and Lord Dunmore had probably all warmed themselves in the hot springs of Sarhad and camped where was now our guesthouse. The difference was that at the time they would all have completed their Wakhan crossing when they did so; we were just starting.

There was a long discussion over dinner about proposed routes, which was pointless since there were only two possible alternatives and of these the longer, higher, but easier one to the north, remained apparently blocked by snow. Both were four- or five-day journeys to the Little Pamir. My mind was now consumed with the same old fears of the precipices, and I tried to discreetly enquire about such issues; Sheffi, our mountain man, dismissed all my concerns, but I don't think he really understood the problem.

An even longer discussion followed, about our objectives in finding the source of the Oxus. No one had been up the Wakhjir (Wakhan-i-Pamir) valley but they knew where it was. Some talked of Lake Chakmaktin, in the Little Pamir as a source of the river, and even suggested that it emptied westwards, in the same direction as the Sarhad Oxus, rather than east towards China, which couldn't be the case, unless it was like the Sonle Lap in Cambodia, and changed direction at different times of the year. However this reflected some of the 19th-century theories, so maybe the explorers had obtained their information from the Wakhis lower in the Wakhan.

It was a happy party for dinner. My altitude fatigues were improving; Dillon and Sheffi were making friends; Anthony was holding court from the comfort of his sleeping bag. This time dinner was a much more communal affair.

Very early next morning we gathered the team together. We were altogether twenty-three men, seventeen horses, and a donkey: the three of us, Anthony, Dillon and myself, each with a horse and a minder, the three guides Sakhi, Nadir and Sheffi, and their horses, and the rest were cooks and porters. The donkey belonged to an old man with a huge black turban; he had grown to look and behave a bit like his donkey. For many days I was unsure whether he was part of our party or just there for the ride.

Quite what eleven pack horses could be carrying was never clear to me, but remarkable things would appear from the saddle packs from time to time, such as an immense watermelon one lunch time when the temperature had risen to over 110F (44C). The expedition could have been mounted with half, or even a quarter the number of people. But the caravan, and our team, were also our passports and our contribution to the Wakhis. Most of the Wakhan valley villages had contributed a man to our team and for them it was a privilege, a diversion and a source of valuable income. We were in effect paying our dues to the community, and we were looked after with every possible care in return.

The caravan set off due east for the Wakhan Range barrier. After an hour or so there was one last village, more of a compound that held humans and animals together. It was more than half a mile away, but within a few moments of our arrival children of all sizes overwhelmed us with greetings, and a deep and excited interest in everything we had, and did. They then rushed back down the hill, with tiny legs beetling over the bouncy turf, and reappeared with armfuls of flat bread and yoghurts. They were rewarded in turn with dates, apricots and other goodies from our supplies.

All three of us eschewed the horses, as we still wanted to make most of the expedition by foot. The only way for lowlanders to walk at altitude is as slowly as possible, with very small steps. I was taught in Bhutan, and on Aconcagua in Chile, to use steps that are no longer than one's foot; it may sound tedious, but it works. However this time, our determination to walk did not last long, as the steepness increased. Anthony, who had been a regular horseman most of his life, soon mounted. I lasted much longer but got aboard when there was a deep river to cross and remained mounted for much of the day. Dillon refused all entreaties from the horsemen, and was still climbing two or more hours later, when we were nearing what we thought to be the top of the Dalez Pass, our first objective. When this turned out to be yet another false crest, he finally succumbed, and then the pattern was set for what would increasingly become a horseback adventure. Although Dalez was as high as any pass on the journey, it was one of the easiest to ascend, as its saddle is reached through a dried up rocky watercourse, rather than an exposed climb up the side of the mountain.

The top re-opens a vista of the Oxus valley where the river emerges from its mountain imprisonment and, as Curzon says, suns itself luxuriantly on the terraced fields and many-fibred streams of the wide watery plain.

The pass opened out into wide, rolling grasslands; or what we first thought were grasslands, but the air was full of a pungent, familiar scent, that I could not place at first. Dillon guessed, rightly, that it was wild thyme, and when we got closer we could see the small gnarled leaves, with their little purple flowers set in the green foliage. Wild thyme, and other Alpine plants would be our fragrant carpet for most of the flatlands that we were to cross.

My altitude sickness began again near the top of the pass. We stopped at midday on a very windy upland meadow, and waited for ages, whilst no lunch, or even a cup of tea arrived, despite several cooks and assistants working on fires and stoves behind wind shelters. I was increasingly irritated, and eventually lost patience with the team and my own discomfort and just set off alone down the other side of the pass. Before long I noticed that Sheffi was following. Sheffi, who had assumed the role of chief steward on the trip, is a mutton of a man, and always had a smile on his face. He knew twelve words of English, and used them in varying order in each sentence, most of which he rehearsed in stage whispers before loosing them on his nearest victim. He always seemed to expect congratulations for this linguistic achievement, which this time, in my grumpiness, I had no intention of giving. It never mattered to Sheffi, how obviously irritated I was by him; he would still do everything in his power to help and support me, which made me feel even worse. With brindled grey beard, moustache, and straggled hair appearing from beneath his scarf and cap, he was our sheepdog, our mascot.

He followed me at a safe distance, bearing my food and tea. It later emerged that the kitchen team had wanted to make a great, and impressive effort for this first meal, and planned chipped potatoes cut into crinkly shapes and cooked with the dedication of Heston Blumenthal. This explained the wait. But still disgruntled, I took no notice of Sheffi and continued on, down the mountain, following what I knew to be our route.

I descended for maybe forty minutes, with a growing sense of dread. Gone were the winding tracks across the thyme covered hill; instead, what confronted me was a steep valley, with a fast river, and beyond, a sheer brown wall. No other exit; no other way than towards what I had least wanted to see, a small fluttering ribbon of a goat path, or pari, apparently without end, crossing the whole exposed face.

Down by the river were three herders, with six yaks of varying sizes, they seemed to be residing there for a while, as they had a fire and bedding material. I sat down with my back to the horror confronting me, and tried to imagine that I was somewhere else, and then, when that failed, I began to fashion fail-safe excuses as to why I had to turn back and leave my companions.

Sheffi finally realised my distress, but it was probably inexplicable to him, a mountain man by breeding. He said: "Bad path horses, you walk" or something like that, and my hitherto mental certainty that four-footed horse equals sure footed travel evaporated.

But he came to the rescue in two ways; first by all but lifting me onto a yak to ford the river. The shock of being on this animal, after just getting used to the horse, let me forget, for a while, the climb to come. Riding a yak is like sitting on the roof of a black Ford Transit with horns.

Then he virtually pushed me up the track. He put his hands on my bum and back, while I concentrated all my energy on staring hard at the stones beneath my feet, avoiding even the merest glance to the right, and the chasm that I could all too easily imagine. Afterwards I could recall every dusty stone, every smooth rock-hold and every tremulous step.

Eventually we reached the top, and even then, I carried on walking, silently, until there was no chance of my looking back. I couldn't get out of my head Wilfred Thesiger's comment, to Eric Newby and Hugh Carless, quoted at the end of *A Short Walk in the Hindu Kush*: "What a pair of pansies, you are". I also suspected that Dr Alex Duncan would soon be leading his wife and four small children on or off yaks up very similar cliff faces without any concern at all.

It took a while to calm my nerves, and concentrate, and by then we were well down the other side and the others had caught up with us. I hardly noticed that we had rejoined the Oxus. Some two thousand or so feet below, it was booming, blue for once in the sunlight, rather than its usual grey. This stretch must have been one of the most magnificent sights along the whole length of the river; the gorge, where the Wakhan Oxus grows. I had hardly noticed; I was pleased to be still standing. I think we were all cowed but unbloodied by the cliff experience, and did not talk much about it. I was tired when we arrived at the stop, and I used the wrong method of dismounting; I should have discarded both stirrups and swung my legs over as normal, but I dismounted on the right stirrup, my foot got caught and I fell on my shoulder. The whole party saw me thrown amongst the tussocks with a thud, and receive a very painful shoulder for my troubles. Not for the last time, they must have been wondering what brought this apparently ill-suited team to the altiplano fortress of the Little Pamir.

We camped by the river having descended again the whole height of the Dalez Pass. There was small a stream behind us, and shelter for a fire. The team set up an open fronted, canvas kiosk as a loo for us, with some amusement. I never did discover in two weeks on the hills, where our team went, or when, for that purpose.

Dillon, Anthony and I had a single yellow tent each, although I believe that we had been expected to share. This meant that the long suffering Sheffi was under the stars much of the time. Evening and lunch were times when the three of us could get together and chat. Much of the day we were necessarily separated, as rarely could two people, or horses walk side by side in the mountains, so we spent much of the day silently watching the slow passing grandeur of the Wakhan massif around us, and the Hindu Kush immediately to the south. We would start as a group but very soon string out, to the extent that we were half an hour or so apart in places, but closed up again at steep or difficult places.

Dillon was concerned to know every detail of our plans, our environment and our companions. He gathered the names, provenance, and ages of the whole team; he tried to communicate with as many as possible and to find out all he could of them, and their way of life. Anthony spent hours writing his diary, but otherwise seemed unconcerned to be too much involved with planning and logistics; he let events move him on and seemed the most relaxed of the three of us. Film makers would have cast Dillon as the sheriff, and Anthony the cowboy. Both reflected these characteristics in their dress; Dillon, was well turned out in khaki, or blue drill shirt, neat trousers, wide brimmed, clean bush-hat over moustache, dark glasses. He had trekking sticks and a GPS in hand, the latter always in use, for location and altitude readings. Anthony on the other hand, wore T shirt, short sleeves, floppy sun hat, and jeans, with spare clothing tied around his waist and falling over the flanks of his grey white trekking mare, a much more lively and adventurous animal than either of ours.

There is no food source in the remote interior of the Wakhan other than by killing a mountain sheep, or fishing, both of which we eventually did. The Kirghiz diet derives almost exclusively from their livestock and the little that they can trade with the Wakhis. As a result they are prone to rickets from vitamin D deficiency. Most of the supplies came with us. Amongst them were boxes of liberated American army rations, in large individual brown packets, with names such as Jambalaya, or Meat Loaf. They were like little food factories on their own; one parcel contained twenty seven different items including three different sauces for the main course, five different condiments, tooth picks, plastic utensils of every description, tiny Mars bars, chewing gum, sugar and gastric pills. The principal dish was in a container that chemically heated itself when a small amount of water was added. These were a source of unending fascination to the Afghans, who explored each sachet with amazement, and laughed at the weird tastes of 'our American guests'. These are apparently the required diet of service personnel. Anthony, Dillon and I had the Afghan food; much the same for breakfast, lunch and dinner; flat bread, tea, yak butter, sugar, beans, and oatmeal porridge. It was the Wakhis who wanted to eat the army rations.

It seemed an opportunity missed to issue Texas-produced rations for the troops in a country as agriculturally rich as Afghanistan. Local production would have been more in keeping with the new relationship that was developing between the native Afghans and the foreign troops. By then in the fifth year of the US-led forces' involvement in the complex war politics of Afghanistan attitudes in large parts of the military had greatly changed. The new thinking was expressed in 2008 by Admiral Mike Mullen, Chairman of the Joint Chiefs of Staff (as quoted by Greg Mortensen): "We cannot kill our way to victory.....nor can we capture hearts and minds. We must engage them; we must listen to them, one heart and one mind at a time".

All the time, the Wakhis made light of the conditions, and the terrain. Some almost ran up the hillsides; others trotted happily along singing songs together. They were capable of twice our speed even with loads, though their footwear was primitive... just sandals or old ill-fitting boots. Their enthusiasm and good humour simply never faded, whatever the circumstances.

My own partner/batman did not conform exactly to this mould. He was certainly strong, and would toil all day, but Nose-boy, as he seemed to be called, was very slow in everything he did. He could start half an hour ahead of the rest, and still be last to arrive. He was undeterred, or even unaware of being the butt of the comments of his colleagues, though sometimes they took pity on him and came to share a joke, or make him sing with them. He had a clown's wide round face with huge ears, and usually a rather vacant expression, which I suspect was a reasonable reflection of his general state of mind, and made him look like a not so colourful Mickey Mouse. He was also, as we found out later, much older than all the other horsemen. Nose-boy and I never really established a relationship other than on a purely practical level. His participation in the venture was as an objective observer, and it seemed that nothing would either surprise or excite him.

Anthony's appointed man, Burhannudin, was less than half Nose-boy's age. He spent much more of his time talking to the others, passing up and down the caravan; he looked as if he would soon be the trader or deal-maker amongst them, more a man of the world than the others. There was a sort of pecking order in which the three leaders, Mohammed Nadir, Sheffi and Sakhi, would sit with us to drink tea, whereas the others would cluster round a separate fire. Somehow Burhannudin made it clear that he would be equally at home in either group.

My horse had some of Nose-boy's characteristics. She was very slow and on ascents she would simply stop and wait for a while, so that I was getting left behind. Sometimes she would do this every few metres, irrespective of my initially unpractised efforts to anticipate the problem with a few kicks. Eventually she would jerk forwards again, with no warning. This was a horse with no personality or style. I called her Margaret Beckett after the then British Deputy Prime Minister; both had strong inclinations to the left and liked to travel in caravan.

Some of the rest of the team I was getting to know better. My favourite, even from the first day, was Holecdoc (maybe more like Qaleq Daq, but he was Holecdoc for me). He seemed to be anywhere between 30 and 40; in fact he was 24. He came from a village very near Sarhad. He looked and behaved like the Artful Dodger. He wore a black Mexican style sombrero, a black ragged jacket, more city executive than anorak, and gumboots much bigger than he needed, with no hint of socks. As chief cook, he had some status, but he was far from content with being just the cook; he wanted to be involved with everything. He did not have a load to oversee, and could range along the caravan, which he did with his bounding stride, usually carrying one or even two heavy thermos of ever available tea.

Although it was really Nose-boy's responsibility to ensure that I did not fall off the mountain, Holecdoc was always there when a difficult place was reached, always at my elbow, unobtrusive, but there nonetheless. By the end of the journey I could have kissed him, and given him the family jewels, and Dillon may well have felt the same. It was Holecdoc who would be the first to see that a pack horse was struggling to keep up or had an ill-balanced load, and would stop it and rearrange or lighten the load.

He was, as the Indian Raj officers used to say, exactly the sort of person to take tiger hunting. One afternoon, while crossing a contributary river one of the horses fell off the path on the upstream side, and was being pummelled by the water, against the rocks. Everyone saw what was happening, but it was Holecdoc who took charge, and soon two horsemen were in the freezing water beside it, loosening its loads, and eventually dragging it to the bank, without a word of complaint.

Many days later and back close to Sarhad Holedoc was to introduce me to a toothless aging woman with a highbacked red headdress, her crusty hand holding that of a young girl. It was his mother. One of the great pleasures of the journey was to be able to tell her of my admiration for her son; her proud and happy smile lives with me still.

We woke early the first morning after Sarhad, and started out along the river bank for about half an hour, before we found a bouncy open-slatted bridge. This was the preface to the first of two unpleasant sections. The only possible path was by way of the rock face above the river, maybe no more than eighty to a hundred feet above the roaring water, but eighty to a hundred too much for my comfort. This was quickly followed by a four hour ascent, which was possibly one of the most beautiful parts of the whole river journey, but I saw little of the grandeur of the Oxus gorge. I had not forgotten Curzon's description:

> *"Below the gorge becomes greatly contracted and the Oxus, gaining volume as it descends, foams noisily ... There is in one place a very bad pari, or cliff track, above the river.... Our ponies had to be unladen and pushed and hauled up the rocks, and even so constantly slipped and fell. It is a bad place for their loads, and one of my bags was ripped clean open. Further on we again left the gorge and diverged inland, mounting and descending successive spurs of great steepness and difficulty, down one of which one of our Kirghiz horses slipped and fell, and was killed instantly."*

My most valuable piece of equipment was an old red and gold silk scarf that my father used to wear as a cravat. I had this under my wide brimmed hat, hanging down on the right side of my face, against the precipice, and secured between my teeth. To an onlooker it might appear to be sensible protection against the high altitude sun; in fact it was the purest funk, designed so that all I could see was the mountainside to the left and to the front of me, so even the temptation to look right was avoided.

It was a steep section, but not one of the severest horrors, where horses, donkey and men were pretty much on their own. What made it unpalatable for me was that it was such a very long stretch. If I knew the end of the chasm was close, then I could feel a little better, but here the pari, on the rare occasions when I allowed myself a glance forward and upward, offered no release at all. Most of the time I could see the horses in front, and in particular Dillon's grey. Dillon was probably even less comfortable with horses than me, but he looked very much the horseman, always riding with a straight back. He seemed to be in control. So I did not immediately understand what was happening when I saw all four of his horse's feet start to slide sideways down the mountain. He was close behind two other horses when he started to go. One moment he and horse were vertical, and formed an acute angle with the mountainside, the next they were parallel with it, and slipping away. If it had been on any of the really steep sections we'd traversed, the horse would have gone, and maybe Dillon with it, though he seemed to slide up off the saddle with some skill, so he might have been able to hold on somewhere. From where I was watching, I just expected them both to fall off the edge, but of course it was Holecdoc who was, as usual, in the right place to turn and hold Dillon, while the horse used a foreleg as an ice axe, steadied himself and recovered his balance. I suspect that for once we, the three lowlanders, were not the only ones relieved by the time we reached the summit.

By the evening we reached Langar (a much used name in the Pamir). Langar is still exactly as described by Curzon 112 years before. The route had taken us far from the river gorge again, which had become very much more contracted, and too precipitous to allow even a pari or track across the face. We camped above the same crumbling riverside tombs, or small shacks that Curzon had found. One was flying a ragged red flag, an incongruous hint of habitation, in an otherwise deserted country. There was a fierce wind but the night sky was one of those in which the stars filled every available space, and were at touching distance.

Across from the tombs was the river, now narrow, grey and fast. It had squeezed into a defile with steep, but rounded cliffs to the south. There was very little precipitation here, so the mountainsides are often traversable in winter, when even the strong river would be frozen.

There were some ibex high above us, which Anthony had the energy to stalk. The porter's camp seemed to be in party mood, partly because I had given them fire crackers and sparklers that miraculously had survived various airline security checks. Maybe for some of porters the evening was enlivened or relaxed, by smoking opium; several of them were users, if not addicts.

The next day was another of physical toil for horses and horsemen, and emotional toil for us, as steep path up followed steep path down. We woke early and started out along the river bank for about half an hour before we were advised to dismount and attack what seemed to be called the Snake Pass, and with good reason. A succession of switchback turns ascended maybe two thousand feet opening onto a wide hillside with more bush and scrub than we had seen for a while. It is hard to gauge relative angles of ascent and descent when one is loath to look away from the ground immediately afoot but for sure the Snake Pass was easier than the previous day's paths because one's eyes are naturally looking straight ahead into rather than down the mountain. Fortunately it did not occur to me then how different it would be on the way back.

The most difficult times for me were when the Oxus was raging, loud through the gorge, many hundreds of feet below. For hours the route would meander far from the water, then a turn around a rock boulder, and half the world opened into a cavern. The waters' roar echoed up the hillside giving teeth and substance to the void.

During the afternoon we came upon the first Kirgiz nomad camp. It was in the process of being dismantled, to move on. There were about twenty yurts, and a hundred animals. Whole yurts were being loaded onto yaks.

The Kirghiz women wore bright red and green dresses, with extended fez, or turbaned headdresses. As we approached the outriders of their moving caravan, they quickly rode away, and waited for us to pass. We couldn't tell if this was shyness or antagonism, until we discovered that the Kirghiz only ride stallions, while the Wakhi tend to ride mares, and therefore avoid each other to reduce the chance of trouble between their mounts.

The Kirghiz camp indicated that we were approaching the end of our seventy kilometre traverse of the Wakhan Massif. For a day or more, I had been waiting, longing to be through the mountains, and imagined at every corner, that a vista of the wide-open Little Pamir would unfold. That was the prize that was awaited…a prize that most mountain climbing misses. Mountaineers climb exposed and difficult pitches; their reward is often another problem with a nasty name like Death Bivouac. The summit is the end with a great view and then a climb down. That is not enough. Adventure is a childish pursuit and seeks childish rewards. C. S. Lewis's wardrobe did not open onto another suburban hallway; the door in the Secret Garden did not reveal another vegetable patch. When we climb the beanstalk we want the excitement Jack had. That, in the Pamir, is what you get.

Eventually, and with inching slowness, it happened. It is not that we were through the mountains, so much as the mountains just flattened out, and there in front of us was the Little Pamir. For once it was almost as I had imagined, maybe five miles wide, an empty, welcoming plateau at the Roof of the World.

At the far end, and still out of sight were the mountains that were the Chinese frontier, to the left Tajikistan and the Big Pamir, where we had been a week before, at Syr Kul; over to the south west would be the Wakhan-i-Pamir (Wakhjir river valley) where we would seek the Ice Cave, and beyond that, the northern tip of the Karakorum, not far from where I stood back in 1986, looking towards the Wakhan, from the top of the Khunjerab Pass.

A few more hours of aching backs, bottoms and thighs, and we were in sight of what were almost the only permanent structures in the inner Wakhan: the tombs of Bozai Gumbaz. It is a compound of four or five mud brick, domed tombs, about eight feet high. They are too small for habitation and could only be for ceremonial or memorial use.

This was the very apex of the Wakhan. This was Matthew Arnold's 'cradle in the High Pamere'. Normally the problem with seeing the world's great mountains is that the closer you get the less you can see, but not so in the Pamirs, whose high altitude plateaux could have been designed as viewing platforms for mountain ranges. The vista down this valley was so startling it could have halted a cavalry charge. The 'Roof of the World' is neither jagged nor forbidding; its features are smooth breasts and thighs. This is landscape as unadorned sculpture. There are no trees or bushes; it is too high; there are no power lines or human detritus; there is nothing to spoil the sweep of the basin, and the soft crests that make up the wide cuttlefish-shaped valley, that should lead to the Ice Cave. The mellow greens, yellows and warm browns of the slopes are broken only by the curling sparkle of the Little Pamir River from the east…all resting in an Aegean blue sky, so broad that it seems to be at once above, beside, and almost underneath. It is the size of the landscape which is its grandeur; a horse or a yak, or a human being is nothing more than an insignificant insect on the canvas of the Pamir, surrounded by the Hindu Kush and Karakorum. This is topography seen through celestial binoculars. It is the Pamir for which even those masters Curzon and Younghusband failed to properly prepare us. Years of anticipation, months of planning, and the long arduous days of access now made glorious sense. I knew exactly why I'd come. I could hear the soaring finale to Das Rheingold; Wagner must have been here to write it, and to understand whence the Gods ascended. For this surely is the road to Valhalla, the Half Way House to Heaven.

Sir Francis Younghusband and colleagues on his 1904 Lhasa expedition

CHAPTER TWELVE

Younghusband Dines with the Russians

It was here at Bozai Gumbaz, at the centre of the Little Pamir that the single most famous incident of the whole Great Game era took place, and established the reputation of the young Francis Younghusband. What became known as the Great Game had developed over the previous half century, but it was in the late 1880s and '90s that it came to the forefront of public consciousness, and of geopolitical importance. A catalyst was the return of Tory Government under the Russophobe Prime Minister, Lord Salisbury, in August 1886. Francis Younghusband was then twenty three, and an ambitious Lieutenant in the Indian Army. He had joined Sandhurst in 1881. In May 1882 he passed out with honours, and was commissioned into the King's Dragoon Guards, then stationed at Meerut in India, where they had recently been involved in the second Afghan War, in which Francis's elder brother, George, had won a medal. Francis was at this age intense, intelligent, humourless and highly religious. He was small, no more than five feet five inches and very much wished he was taller.

His life, on arrival with the Regiment, was disappointing, and boring. He wrote to his sister Emmie: "The talk in the mess is very bad; nothing but scandal about the people in the station". Like so many young officers he had come with dreams of immediate military achievements, heroics for the Empire, promotion and glory in uniform. Instead he was thrown into a society of rich young men with few cares, many servants, and little to compete for, except the quality of their polo ponies, and little to look forward to except a visit to the Rag, which was the Regimental brothel, staffed by Indian women, and paid for out of the Canteen fund. His only real friend in the mess died of fever in August of his first year.

It was not only the young man's romantic notions, developed from his reading of the history of military and civilian exploration in Asia, that made him long for something more exciting; it was also the influence of his uncle, and hero, Robert Shaw. Shaw lived in Dharamsala, as a tea planter, but had been lured north in 1868. He travelled across the Himalaya from Leh into Chinese Turkestan to the north, where Yakoub Beg had proclaimed from Kashgar the Kingdom of Kashgaria, a challenge to all three of the surrounding Empires. He reached Yarkand after three months, and eventually became the first known European to reach Kashgar, still one of the prime objectives of all Asian travel. Today this market city is as cosmopolitan in its own way, as London is, but hard to reach and almost as far from any sea as is possible on earth. It is a city of intrigue, rumour, news and colour, even though its Chinese masters still think of it as little more than a place to exile their less successful political officers. In 1868 it would have been even more alluring, and exciting to Robert Shaw and his companions. Shaw was joined in Kashgar soon afterwards, by the equally intrepid George Hayward, who had been sent there on a mission from the Royal Geographical Society. Both were then imprisoned by the nervous Yakoub Beg. They were released a few months later and sent back to India, with messages of goodwill for the Viceroy. Yakoub Beg wanted at least to pretend that he was on India's side against any threat of a possible Russian invasion.

Within 10 years both were dead. Hayward was decapitated by Dacoits in Dardistan, (inspiring the Henry Newbolt poem 'He Fell Amongst Thieves') and Shaw died of fever in Mandalay while exploring Burma, by then, as a fully enrolled Political Agent of the Government.

Younghusband took time off to re-trace some of his uncle's travels from Ladakh in 1884, but it was not until 1885 that he managed to become, at last, part of the little spy-ring that made up the players of the Great Game. The gamers were really only part-time spies, under the general umbrella of Sir Charles Macgregor, the head of intelligence for the Indian Army. They were at considerable risk, as they were never officially recognised by their masters, were usually in disguise, and were almost always sent to places where they could not have been rescued.

Macgregor recognised in Younghusband, an ideal candidate for this branch of intelligence, and soon Younghusband had proposed his own mission, though not in the expected area of the North West frontier, Hindu Kush and Karakorum, but in Manchuria, in China's unknown North East. His reasoning was that the recent establishment of Russian protectorate status in Korea, had effectively left Manchuria encircled and therefore very much at risk to Russian imperialism.

Their journey is described in the first part of Younghusband's book *Into The Heart of a Continent*. The second and most memorable part, describes his return journey across China to India. This is one of the supreme travel adventure stories of the 19th or any other century.

It came about because when they returned to Peking, Younghusband's superior officer Captain Mark Bell VC was there planning to try to be the first European to cross China from the East. Younghusband approached him and asked if he could accompany him on the journey. He probably asked, with some trepidation, as Bell was a notoriously difficult man. At first Bell agreed then, the night before they were due to depart, Bell said that he had changed his mind and could not see the point of Younghusband joining him. However if he wanted to go he should take a parallel journey through the Gobi Desert and he would meet him in Hami on the far side of the great expanse of what was thought to be the empty wastes.

Somehow Younghusband's party did cross the Gobi, finding their way without much idea of where they were going, from watering hole to well, sometimes as much as a hundred miles apart. It took seventy days to traverse the 1,250 miles of desert.

When they got to Hami, there was no sign of Bell, but after enquiries he found that another 'round eye' had indeed been there, a week or two earlier. He had stayed an afternoon and then departed again. Younghusband continued to his uncle's city of Kashgar, now back in the control of a Chinese puppet ruler.

At Kashgar, the Tien Shan frames the north western view, and the route south to Yarkand passes the great peaks of Kongur and Mustagh Ata. Younghusband was beginning to feel that his objective was within his grasp, but he had still to traverse the Himalaya Karakorum, the world's most fearsome physical frontier.

The record of his descent of the Mustagh Pass, and arrival amongst the astonished inhabitants of Askole (now one of the starting points for expeditions to K2 and the peaks of Concordia in the Pakistan Karakorum) is one of the classics of Victorian travel literature. Patrick French, his biographer, wrote that the descent of the Pass would assume "a mythical importance in Younghusband's career…the rite of passage, the crossing of the watershed, the epiphany of ice, convinced him that he had a special purpose in the world".

They arrived at the top of the Mustagh after following the course of the Yarkand river, on the written instructions of Bell; maybe Bell knew what was in store for them, and to some extent, was hoping to inspire Younghusband's failure. They were at nineteen thousand feet, cold, uncertain of their route, and very apprehensive about their safety, and were confronted by a sheer precipice of ice. They had only leather shoes and jackets, no mountain equipment of any sort. Younghusband had only ever heard of the techniques of climbing, and the others had no idea what to do. It seemed that this was the end of their journey, and a very ignominious end. There was no route to India from China, and that would have to be his report to Bell, and to Macgregor.

But as Younghusband stood and contemplated his predicament, Wali his guide, mistook his silence for stoicism and, "knowing that no Englishman would turn back" set off down the precipice, hacking his way out onto an ice ledge. Following his lead, they knotted what rope they had with turbans and belts and started down the cliff creating holds out of chinks of ice for their bootless feet. When all six were on the face together,

Drogba, the caravan leader, panicked and started to scramble back. Younghusband in pure, cold fear, pretended to be composed, and in charge of himself, and somehow drove them all on to relative shelter, across the slope. There was worse to come however, when they were confronted by an ice wall that was almost vertical. Still they managed to find some rock holds, to which, when they could, they attached themselves using a makeshift rope. Six hours later, they had conquered the pass; the next day they skirted the great Baltoro Glacier, and two days later they were in Askole, arriving from the North, as none had done before them. This as Sven Hedin, the Swedish master explorer of Chinese Turkestan said, "was the most difficult and dangerous achievement ever in these mountains".

His diaries reveal Younghusband as both grandiose and at the same time reflective as he looked back at the Mustagh Range: "My feelings can only be understood by those who have penetrated the mountain solitudes of the Himalaya and stood alone, as I now did, in the innermost recesses of the mightiest mountains in the world; separated from the haunts of civilisation…and far from the abodes of even the wild and woolly hill-men of the Himalayas. Alone, where no white men have ever set foot, where all is snow and pure ice, white and unblemished, and where even the rustle of a single leaf, the faintest murmur of a stream, or the hum of the smallest insect, rose to break the spell of calm repose which reigned around". Here are the seeds of what was to become his preoccupation in middle and old age, as a seeker of spiritual enlightenment in Northern India, a forerunner perhaps of the hippy pilgrimages to India in the later 20th century.

After the trans-China adventure his ambition was to get to Wakhan and the Pamir. He finally received permission for the mission soon after his twenty-seventh birthday in 1890.

He was joined on the journey by George Macartney, who was to spend the next seventeen years as the British Consul in Kashgar. Instead of going directly to the Wakhan they went north to Chinese Turkestan in the direction of Yarkand. They diverted into the Alai Mountains of modern Tajikistan, to investigate the rumours of Dragon lake, and then back to Kashgaria, and eventually Kashgar itself. There then followed a low period for Younghusband. He was to be nine months in Kashgar, wily and devious Petrovski, the Russian consul. Petrovski was an experienced diplomat and he was winning the war of influence with the Chinese. Younghusband was an adventurer and a soldier; he knew little yet of diplomacy and politics, and anyway, was cut off by a four-month mail delay from any advice from India. He was well out of his depth, and it was with great relief that he rode south out of Kashgar, towards his real goal, the Wakhan. He was in the company only of a handful of servants, and the young Lieutenant Davison, who had arrived in Kashgar, and attached himself to the party. Davison seemed to fawn upon both his superior officer and his reputation.

He could have taken a number of possible more northerly routes into Wakhan but chose to go via the Wakhjir Pass, right at the apex of the Pamir Knot, where the five ranges meet: Pamir, Hindu Kush, Himalaya, Kun Lun and Karakorum. This is the watershed between Indus and Oxus, as Younghusband writes; "if any point is the true Heart of Asia, this is it".

Descending the Wakhjir Pass they advanced up the wide Pamir along the river to Bozai Gumbaz. He found there a small party of Cossacks from the forward base in Murgab, which confirmed the fears about Russian designs on the area. However Younghusband still considered their presence as "a bit of a brag, from which they would soon withdraw". The commander was his friend Captain Yanov, with whom he dined, and he was most impressed by the Russian victuals. "They always seem able to produce soups and stews. They also had vegetables and relishes together with two different types of wine and brandy". They dined in a tiny open tent admiring, as we were to 120 years later, the grand expanse of the upper Wakhan as they drank alternately the health of the Tsar and Queen Victoria. The two explorers were bound much closer, by their common interests and experiences in the Pamir, than ever they were divided by nationality.

However, the next day, more Cossacks arrived, and Younghusband's friend came to his camp in apparently different mood, and required him immediately to leave 'Russian territory'. As the odds were about two against fifty, he had little alternative but to agree, under severe protest. He knew that the orders came from above Yanov, and he carefully assured

Yanov that despite his protests he held no grudge against his friend, and 'begged the Captain and his officers to stay for supper'. Shaking with emotion, according to Younghusband, Yanov hugged him, and apologised for having to behave 'like a police official'.

A runner was sent back to Gilgit to inform the British of the Russian claims. When the news reached London, the reaction, after initial puzzlement as to where in the world Bozai Gumbaz might be, was fierce; so fierce that the Russian Foreign Minister genuinely believed that London expected war. The Russians started backing down and disowning Yanov's actions, though privately he was decorated by the Tsar. The British Government was also quietly backpedalling, and disowning the hothead-edness of their representative, as neither government was in the mood for a skirmish in that area, whatever their public posturings might suggest. Nevertheless when the confrontation became general knowledge, Bozai Gumbaz became as well known and talked about an outpost as Gibraltar and the Falkland Islands would ever be.

Younghusband left the Wakhan as commanded by Yanov, using much the same route as he had come. He stayed for six weeks up in the Pamir Knot, and there found "on the Oxus side of the watershed …a small lake, about three-quarters of a mile in length, three of its sides were formed by cliffs of ice, the terminal walls of glaciers, out of which flowed a small stream which joins the Panj branch of the Oxus, at Bozai Gumbaz". At this time he made no attempt to suggest that this could be the source of the Oxus, though it would have been a reasonable claim. He stayed on the Roof of the World, setting up camp by the Kilik Pass, whence he proceeded to establish a small network of spies around the area, designed to report on any Russian activity. There was none.

The 1891 incidents confirmed Younghusband's public reputation in his role as youthful adventure hero of the Empire, standing up for British rights where they were most threatened. Now he was Younghusband of Wakhan more than of the Mustagh Pass. The legend and mystery of this little strip of land had deepened. It had bemused and attracted adventurers for centuries, now it also befuddled politicians.

Anthony in front of Bozai Gumbaz

CHAPTER THIRTEEN

Up the Wakhan-i Pamir

This virgin land where Younghusband met Yanov was now ours to borrow for a few days, although we were not alone. Near the camp and a little to the north towards Tajikistan and the Big Pamir, was a Kirghiz nomad camp. That evening we bought from them a sheep. It was killed with a little ceremony by the team, and was to be an important part of our food for many days to come.

This is Kirghiz, not Wakhi, country. These Kirghiz are amongst the very few true nomads left in the world. They maybe called Kirghiz, possibly because they speak the language, but they do not have the slightly Mongol looks of many native Kirghiz and Kazakhs. They are reputed to be descended from the Tuva nomads from the Siberian steppe, who had migrated to the Pamir 700 years ago and roamed then freely for centuries to and from Pamir and China as far maybe as the Kun Lun. The closing of the frontiers hurt even the nomads and a hiatus ensued in which many tried to cross the Hindu Kush and live in North Pakistan. Few found it easy and in 1982 a large group, maybe as much as fifty percent of the population, journeyed west and were eventually given asylum in Anatolia. The ones that remain are enclosed in the cul de sac, connected to the world by nothing, supported and housed by nothing other than yurts, surviving on a mini-trade with the Wakhis and living at the very edge of sustainability. For them Sarhad and the Wakhi villages to the west represent wealth and civilisation compared with their own lot. These, the few hundred nomadic horsemen of the Little Pamir were to be our guides in what might be the most isolated and inaccessible area of human habitation on earth, or in the words of Greg Mortensen "a place so austere, so remote that it may not seem as much like the end of the road as the end of the world itself".

The nomads were preparing to move. However we understood that they had an agreement with the Wakhi from west, down the corridor, that they had the right to provide all horses and yaks for travellers in the Little Pamir area. We, though, were finally getting used to our mounts, and were reluctant to learn new animals at this stage of the journey. Also we knew that their mounts would be stallions and there would surely be conflict amongst the horses.

There was a long parley between the two groups. It seemed to be mainly posturing, since the nomads were clearly not in a position to supply fifteen or more horses, and needed all the transport they had for their current migration. Their yurts were being dismantled around us. But a discussion about whose horses to use was certainly not to be undertaken lightly. These are men for whom horses are central to their lives. They represent their wealth and status; the Kirghiz nomad male and his horse are almost a single being. A Montana cowboy is less attached to his horse than these Kirghiz.

The Kirghiz were represented by the local village leader, a thin, wizened man with a woolly hat, who looked 55 but was probably in his 40s. A compromise was agreed whereby we'd take on just four Kirghiz horsemen, and leave four of ours at the camp, for our return.

We were invited to breakfast in the Kirghiz camp, which they had prepared in advance, for our arrival. Three generations of Kirghiz were there to watch us; grandfathers with faces wrinkled like root ginger, bearded fathers wearing check shirts, or Russian army surplus jackets, and a whole kindergarten of various sized children, with runny noses, red sun-damaged cheeks, and coalminers black hands in every variety of Central Asian costume: Afghan embroidered waistcoats, baggy red Chinese trousers with bandana belts, and full length Kirghiz cloaks for the girls... The headgear was equally multicultural: traditional green and gold fez type caps, and wool bobbles for younger men; multicoloured turbans, like ice cream cones, or steppes' ear muffs for the older men. The younger women had shawls draped over their Kirghiz caps, white for the unmarried and red for the married. We sat on rugs in one of the last standing yurts. It was about six metres across, with an embroidered hanging to separate the work area from the reception area. We had golden cream, and salty yak butter tea into which we dunked flat hard bread.

It may be that messages about the previous evenings' discussions had been passed to the overall Kirghiz nomad chief, for he arrived that morning. He and I exchanged gifts, our trinkets for their bread and yoghurts, with easy going ceremony. But then a long argument started between him, supported by others with Nadir and some of our team. This went on and on. Sakhi explained that the previous days' discussion had not been settled; the Kirghiz did not want us to go any further without using their horses. These were still away from the camp, and would not be back for three or more days, which meant we'd have to stay there until they arrived. From time to time the participants just chatted, disregarding their differences, and then took up their arguments again, quite animatedly. Then the Kirghiz would withdraw into a sort of informal *jirga*, or council session in which issues are discussed endlessly over cups of tea until some unanimity is reached. It must have been reached as slowly it became clear that we were to be allowed to leave and that the Kirghiz had sufficiently made their point that travel decisions in, and control of the area was theirs, and that we were subject to such rules as they wished to impose. More presents were offered, and accepted; more children had bangles around their wrists and wives were adorned with Southall necklaces, and we were able to leave.

We had travelled by then about eighty percent of the length of the Wakhan Corridor and reached the divide. The route north east is along the length of the Little Pamir, but we had to go south east into the Wakhir river landscape. We set off ahead of the horses towards the lush grassland around the Little Pamir River. The landscape was very similar to that of the Scottish highlands; take away the towns, and villages, raise it by twelve thousand feet and this could almost be Deeside. The river slices a neat green swathe through rough, tussocked country, sparkling in the morning sun. It was thirty to seventy metres wide, and cleaner than anything we had seen since the uplands of the Alai, in Kyrghizia. This was the river that had its source in the hills above the Little Pamir and which 19th-century Russian and other explorers considered to be the true source of the Oxus. (Marked B on the map on pages 8/9)

Just south of here was the confluence of the Little Pamir river with the Wakhjir, and therefore the heart of the whole venture, that had begun months before, sitting at my computer console in Chobham. It was already clear that then the primacy of the Wakhjir branch at this time of year, would be hard to dispute. I questioned the Kirghiz about this, via Sakhi, who had now developed an intellectual interest in the river himself. The Kirghiz and Wakhi did not seem at all surprised at this debate about the river source. Indeed, they all had opinions that were worth considering. On the matter of the Little Pamir *v* the Wakhjir however there was little dispute. The big, bright, tumbling brook from the Pamir was generally smaller that its grey chalk neighbour that came, we expected, from Curzon's Ice Cave, even though the latter disguised its size by spreading itself across a wide basin. As one Kirghiz put it: "The clean one can always be crossed by horse, whereas the Wakhjir sometimes can only be crossed by strong horse, and sometimes not at all."

The Wakhjir valley is two to three kilometres across, at river level. The valley floor is about thirteen thousand feet and the peaks around fifteen to seventeen thousand. For the walker, in such a huge landscape, progress seems infinitesimal, the scenery changes so slowly. Only by taking a sighting against the distant Bozai Gumbaz could one discern progress. Around midday we climbed up to the north, into a small stream valley by three Kirghiz yurts. The view back the way we had come, with sun behind it was as beautiful as anything we'd ever seen, chalk river gave way to moraine, which in turn transformed into lush banks, then a mild, green, thyme-covered prairie, and in the far distance, the hazy, rocky uplands, and eventually the snow covered, granite peaks, a horizon that would daily renew any mountain mans' vows.

There were only women in the Kirghiz yurts, so it took some time to establish communication. When we did, we got a cooking lesson in making flat bread, yogurt and the luxurious yak double cream, from the three assembled generations. During the afternoon a nascent horsemen's revolt about daily distances has to be averted. This surely has been fermented by the Kirghiz arrivals but was never much more than a discussion. However in part it derived from the fact that we were moving down the valley much faster than we had expected and would get close to the end by the next day. This suggested that the paid days might be fewer than had been expected. Instead of camping where we had planned using our Russian military maps, we went another few kilometres eastwards towards what we hoped to the glacial end of the valley.

We camped in a slightly swampy spot, but dined well, as we had a choice of meat or offal from the sheep we'd bought a few days before. The hard mutton offal was a far better choice than the chewy and tasteless meat, but it would have been even better to have been able to accompany it with river cooled beer, or a goblet of Provence red wine and watch the stars through the haze of a smokable weed, but this was Afghanistan, not Bhutan or Nepal.

The Kirghiz had warned us that our route would be interrupted by a river, which was only passable early in the day, before too much snow melt had raised levels, so we camped as close as we could get to it that night, to allow an early crossing the next day. In the event we reached it about 9.30 a.m. and managed to get all loads over without too much trouble other than much shouting at animals and between horsemen.

For two hours we reached along the valley. Nadir, with mountain trained eyes, sighted Marco Polo sheep, the quarry that were as much a draw as the excitement of the Great Game skirmishes in the 19th century.

They were way up on the far side of the valley and very hard to distinguish, but seemed like a message from our predecessors. Still we could not see the end of the Wakhan-i-Pamir, or Wakhjir river valley, and none of us had any idea of what sort of terrain to expect, or how we would eventually reach the Ice Cave. I imagined that we would be climbing up a final few hundred metres of waterfall or rock cliff; Sakhi and Nadir clearly did not think so, as they talked of taking food, for cooking some sort of lunch up there.

The plan was that we should set up camp somewhere from which we would be able to re-cross the awkward river early the next morning after the Ice Cave, if we got there and back. It was about two in the afternoon when we made camp. Nadir chose a camp site where the river was at its widest. Nestling between riverbed and mountainside it was a sheltered, tussocked, flatland, so obvious a campsite that it was not at all unlikely that this very same place would have been chosen by Curzon, on his 1895 journey.

George Nathaniel Curzon, 1st Marquis Keddleston 1859-1925.
Viceroy of India 1898-1905

CHAPTER FOURTEEN

George Nathaniel Curzon and The Ice Caves

It would be surprising if the fame of Younghusband, after his Wakhan adventures had not elicited some jealousy in the thirty-two-year-old Honourable George Nathaniel Curzon. Curzon was the eldest son of Lord Scarsdale, and would later become Marquess of Kedleston, and as Viceroy of India, the second or third most powerful person in the British Empire. He considered that Afghanistan, Central Asia and Russo/British relations in the area to be his territory; he was already Parliamentary Under Secretary for India.

He was by all accounts, aloof, or appeared to be, but this was substantially because an injury sustained while horse riding had left him with severe back pain, which required him to hold himself erect and stiff. He was ambitious, but also very clever. He never doubted that he would assume power in one way or other. But he was not a distant or forbidding man; he was fun, entertaining, and a social contributor, but mainly in circles that he respected, and that was made up of people he felt to be his equal. Foremost amongst these was the group he joined at Oxford: the Souls. Certainly there was an element of intellectual snobbery in the group; members included Arthur Balfour, Herbert Asquith, Alfred Lyttleton, the Tennant sisters, and many of his fellow Balliol men (there were 49 of them in the House of Commons alone). It was like a political pre-cursor of the Bloomsbury set of John Maynard Keynes and Virginia Woolf. Curzon was as establishment as it was possible to be in late 19th-century Britain.

He had been appointed Minister of State in the India office in 1891, but a year later, Gladstone's Liberals had won the election against Salisbury's Tories, and therefore he was out of office. This gave him more time for his travels. The first journeys took him to China, Persia, the Caspian, India, Russia and North Africa. But the journey that was to make his name as traveller and explorer was the one that took him to the Wakhan in 1894.

There were two powerful reasons why Curzon wanted to go to the Wakhan Corridor. Firstly, the area was now well known after the Younghusband exploits; it had travellers' provenance. Curzon was no private traveller; he wanted to visit places which would impress the public when he returned. He cited Richard Burton's wish to find the 'fountains of Oxus' as his inspiration, and set the scene with all the gravitas he could muster:

"To myself also the Oxus, that great parent stream of humanity, which has equally impressed the imagination of Greek and Arab, of Chinese and Tartar, which, from a period of three thousand years ago, has successively figured in the literature of the Sanscrit Puranas, the Alexandrine historians, and the Arab geographers... had always similarly appealed".

Secondly, the issue of where and how the Tsar's armies could get access to India was still a matter of keen military interest, and no one had done a survey of the Hindu Kush and Karakorum passes from that aspect; this gave a legitimate political purpose to the trip, and enabled its financing by the Government of India.

However these reasons were not enough to explain why a man of Curzon's power and ambition should have been out on a very distant scouting expedition, which could have been done instead by any number of Indian army officers or their appointees.

The explanation is not to be found in his official biography however, published soon after his death in 1925; but it shines out from Curzon's own writing and commentary. He was a traveller; he was one of those people who grows at once excited, and content when in the wild, or the unknown. Any excuse is enough to leave, and seek new adventures, to explore the unfamiliar. At home we all look at maps, and conjure places from the romance of the names, but the biggest thrill is the destination itself, and even more, the journey to find it. Curzon never quite said this, but he didn't need to. It is so clearly a genuine and personal longing. When he wrote about places and scenes, he lost his inclination to lecture, and enjoyed himself at last.

It helps that he was a marvellous and descriptive writer. The Victorian era before colour photography or film had had to rely on words alone. Many of those Asian travellers, including Younghusband, Shaw, and later Tillman, were fine writers, but none had the florid, evocative talent of George Curzon. Over a hundred years later, his book is still by far the most detailed, and useful guide to the lower Pamir and Wakhan. The first part of Curzon's report to the Royal Geographical Society in 1895 was our guide book for this 2007 expedition; nothing better exists.

He was sure that it was his responsibility to determine which of the many claimants was the true parent stream, and to advise once and for all time, whether the Wakhan 'is the vulnerable gate of Hundustan', or 'a horrible wilderness, and sure death-trap for invading armies'.

He took the route north from Rawalpindi following the general direction of what would now be the Karakorum Highway. At Hunza he was welcomed by the Mir, who had recently deposed his own brother, with the help of the Indian Government. Curzon, with a masterpiece of delicate insult, describes the brother, Safdar Ali Khan, as "a murderer and fratricide of more than ordinary activity".

The route to the Kilik, the Hunza Valley, he describes as 'one of the worst tracks in the world'. The cultivation and luxuriance of Hunza gave way to the true Karakorum austerity, and the sort of territory that had turned me back from Shimshal in the Karakorum in 1986. In places the path consisted only of artificial ladders, and ledges of brushwood and timber jammed into rock crevices, built out over the gorge. Curzon claimed that during these few days he underwent "the bodily labours of a Parliamentary session, and parted with the superfluous accretions of an entire London season". The main difficulty was fording the swollen rivers; the Hunza men were good swimmers but they were still taken hundreds of yards downstream when trying to transport baggage across the icy creeks, whether alone or aided by inflated goatskins as floatation support.

They continued north to the Kilik Pass (16,300ft) into Chinese Turkestan, where they shot *Ovis Poli* for sport, and then West to take the same Wakhjir Pass as Younghusband had taken three years earlier. Reaching the top of the pass, they saw before them the wide Wakhan-i-Pamir. The descent into the valley was steep and rough. At the base, Curzon did what he claims had not been done before, he turned back east, up the river valley, and it is there that he found the Ice Cave. He provided what was the only evidence, or report, of the Wakhjir source of the Oxus for the next hundred and more years:

"From far above, the main glacier can be seen winding round from the north, or left hand, to the head of the gorge, in which, however its discharge was not visible. Descending to the shingle bed, which varies from 100-350 yards wide, the channel being divided into several branches, I rode up it to the source. There the river issues forth from two ice-caverns in a rushing stream. The cavern on the right has a low overhanging roof, from which the water gushes tumultuously out. The cavern on the left was sufficiently high to admit of my looking into the interior, and within for some distance I could follow the river, which was blocked with great slabs of ice, while there was a ceaseless noise of grinding, crunching, and falling in."

Curzon climbed up the precipitous ice above the cave to view the big glacier, and to understand where the ice formed, and found that there were three glaciers, all converging into one above the ice cave itself.

It was certainly not obvious to him at the time that he had 'found the true source' as he later determined that he had. It appears to have been more by chance than planning, that he had reached the Pamir via the Wakhjir Pass, although he did know that the Little Pamir beyond would be one of his most important destinations for research. It must have been later, after the whole Wakhan journey, that he became convinced this was actually the answer to his quest.

This suited Curzon very well indeed, because first it was a discovery that no one else had made, and second the Ice Cave, as a river source was quite as romantic as a high altitude lake, and far more glamorous than a small hidden spring. So he set out to demonstrate that this was indeed the source, and much of his reports to the RGS, and published work, is devoted to dismissing the arguments in favour of the other possible parent streams: Lake Chakmaktin, the Sarhad branch and the Panj river.

His arguments to support the claims of the Wakhjir River, sourced at the Ice Cave, as the true parent stream are based on the length and volume of the various claimants. He had not visited all the sources and had to rely on reported information about variations in flow between seasons.

The four possibilities then were:

A. Panj River flowing originally from Syr Kul, discovered by John Wood

B. Little Pamir River near Bozai Gumbaz flowing down the Little Pamir from the East towards Sarhad and becomes the Wakhan River after the conjunction (which becomes the Wakhan River after the conjunction with the Wajkir) advocated by 'the Mirza', M. Capus, and the Russians

C. Aksu/Murghab/Bartang branch which flows from Lake Chakmaktin advocated by Lord Dunmore and Colonel Trotter

D. His own discovery of the Ice Cave leading to the Wajkir River

(Marked A, B, C, D on map on pages 8/9)

The first question to be answered ought to be: which is the greater branch at the major confluence, way downstream from the Wakhan at

Vomar Roshan, where the Aksu (D) flows into the combined waters of A,B,C. Curzon relied on the reports of Ney Elias "the only Englishman to have been there (November 1885)", as he wrote. He advised that "from careful inspection and personal fording of both rivers, and minute local inquiries he was able to satisfy himself that the Panj was, all seasons of the year except one, a much more voluminous stream than the Murghab (Aksu)". The exception was June and July when the closer proximity of glacier feeders increased the volume of the Murghab, so that it equated with the Panj. This was a weak argument as he had not been anywhere near Roshan itself, however there were few more reliable witnesses than Ney Elias, who was admired as the premier Asian explorers by almost all his contemporaries. Our own later visit to Roshan in July confirmed that the two rivers did indeed seem to be about the same size; there was no way that either could have been forded at that time of year.

If, as Curzon had concluded the Aksu/Murghab is not the parent stream, then the quest was for the source of the Panj. The choice then lay between the Syr Kul source discovered by Wood and the Wakhan/Sarhad river coming from the Little Pamir.

Curzon simply took the line that Wood was wrong to decide that the northern branch up to Syr Kul was the parent. Somewhat arrogantly, he berated Wood for heeding the advice of local Wakhanis. At a distance in time of more than 50 years, and with no prior knowledge of the area, Curzon still felt confident that Wood made the wrong decision. Instead Curzon insisted that Wood should have turned east up the Wakhan to find the source.

Had Wood and Curzon met they would have argued their respective claims and no doubt, the more forceful Curzon would have at least appeared to have the stronger hand. They might have sat together in Curzon's Viceregal smoking room and fought their corners:

"In choosing the Panj as opposed to the Sarhad branch, Lieutenant Wood, you made an avoidable error. Your own estimate of the respective flows led you to the Sarhad branch; why did you not follow your instinct?"

"I had good reasons, Lord Curzon. The advice of the local Wakhis was that the Panj branch was the greater river. Having never been there, it is hard for you to judge, but I can tell you that both rivers are very wide, so that the confluence is as much as two miles across. One's own eye alone is a poor yardstick, as depth and speed of flow are equally valuable indicators of the parent stream."

"I am surprised that you, as a Naval man, with the experience you already have of the Indus, would rely on local gossip".

"That is exactly what I do. I rely on the local expertise of people whose whole livelihood is bound up with the river. In addition I was able to test speed of flow and temperature. The Panj was nearly twice as fast and colder, the latter being a clear indication that the source was higher."

"I think that you were too much influenced by the theory that the Sarhad River led back to Mastuj, and even Chitral. Had you known as we now do, that the Hindu Kush and Pamir watershed, along the southern boundary of the Wakhan Corridor makes this impossible, you would have taken a different course, one which would have led you eventually, to the Ice Cave, which is the true source of the river".

"In the Pamir conditions, as you know well, vary widely with the season. I understood that during the spate, the Panj grows proportionately greater than the Sarhad".

"I suspect that you were misinformed; it is clear that the Sarhad branch has a much greater catchment area to drain".

Having disposed of the Syr Kul claim to his own satisfaction, the question then remained as to which was the parent stream of the Sarhad/Wakhan river. Was it the Wakhjir river from the Ice Cave, or the Little Pamir River? Curzon has no trouble eliminating the Sarhad branch. As we had already seen at the confluence, it was clear that the Wakhjir is much the bigger, and one has to agree with him, that it is surprising that anyone should have simply disregarded the Wakhjir on that evidence alone. The probability must be that there were significant seasonal differences, which made the judgement call more difficult for those such as 'the Mirza' and M. Capus that had advocated this source.

The elimination of the Little Pamir River as the source left Curzon holding the prize.

It would have been very important to Curzon to prove his point, as otherwise, his discovery of the Ice Cave would have been no more than an interesting geographical curiosity, as opposed to one of the seminal discoveries of the age, as he was to see it. Curzon's book and RGS papers are written as polemics, rather than works of systematic geography. He bowled over his audience with his conviction, and his scholarship. There were doubters, particularly those who had discovered the other claimant streams. Following Curzon's third paper to the RGS in September 1895, there was a remarkable public argument amongst the advocates of the different sources. Almost all the distinguished explorers of Central Asia, other than Ney Elias (unless he was there incognito) and Sir Aurel Stein, were gathered for the event. Lord Dunmore, who had been advised of the event, cried off with a cold, or some such excuse, probably because he did not want to face the vastly greater debating skills of Curzon. Colonel Trotter stood in for him, and made a good case for the Murghab Oxus. Younghusband was there also, and repeated his own claims; effectively saying that if Curzon was right, then he, Younghusband had already found the parent to the parent stream.

But the argument for most commentators had already been won. The other claims were soon forgotten; Curzon's scholarship and diligence had won the day.

CHAPTER FIFTEEN

The Heart of Asia's Mountains

It was 112 years later, and our chance had come to test these arguments.

Our party to go to find Curzon's Ice Cave was reduced to just Dillon, Anthony and me, plus Sakhi, Nadir, Sheffi and the only one of our horsemen, Mirza Mohammed, who claimed to have some prior experience in the valley. He was a tall, strong man, with hands like mill wheels, but harder. He wore a green and gold Kirghiz hat, which he later gave to me as a present. He seemed far too large for his horse and almost dragged his feet along the ground.

We were now travelling east and a little south. Ahead of us would be the place that we know as the very centre of Asia, the apex of the Pamir Knot, where the great mountain chains meet. We began to turn what had to be the last bend in the valley before we'd see the glacier itself. We knew that it should be around 1,000 feet above us if our readings were correct.

Within less than ten kilometres were both Pakistan and Xinjiang. To the left up a steep ridge were the tracks which lead to the Wakhjir Pass, and the Chinese border. This was the very entry point used by Younghusband and Curzon. It was rumoured that there was some trading activity through the pass and that the Chinese had marked their side with a concrete bollard, but no one we met had been there.

We were now, for the first time on the journey, walking along the riverbed itself. The going was as easy as it had been at any stage in the previous ten days. It seemed that all we had to do was walk up the moraine bed to reach our objective. We were clearly reaching for the cul-de-sac that ended in a mountain face barrier that now absorbed almost the whole view. The valley narrowed, and high above us, the face of the glacier slowly emerged. We searched its base by binoculars, looking for the Ice Cave, but it clearly petered out into bare rock, with no sign of a conjunction with the river; it was not even part of the valley. The thought re-occurred that the Ice Cave might not even be there anymore. We continued up the long bend for a while, and then there directly in front of us, there emerged clearly a much bigger glacier, with its base apparently accessible and low. The valley ended abruptly at a wall sliced apart by a central ice field. It led back into the mountain, sloping much more steeply as it rose, and turned south, into Pakistan and the Karakorum. The Ice Cave had to be at the base. For a moment we felt a twinge of disappointment that our target, the prize we'd been dreaming of, should be so easily obtained. But still, at the back of my mind, the question of altitude remained; surely we were still far too low?

And indeed we were, as the altimeter reading confirmed; it was just the breadth of the landscape that confounded both distance and apparent inclination. We must have been climbing all the time, and as we approached closer to the valley end, what had seemed to be a flat grey approach path refocused into jumbled moraine and boulder layers. By then the base of the glacier had disappeared behind hills of shale and stone and the route to the destination was no longer clear.

It was naive to have imagined that the Ice Cave would relinquish its relative virginity so easily. The route ahead now looked difficult; there was no access to the south of the river, as the valley side was black precipitous rock, leading only to the upper part of the glacier. The one apparently simple route was to go straight up the north west bank, above all the moraine jungle. There seemed to be a plateau four hundred feet or so above the valley, which we could use to approach the glacier from the north and then come down into the face of it from above. What was not clear however, was whether or not we would then be met by further barriers, as yet invisible. It was now close to 4 p.m. and it was too late in the day to be attempting something of this uncertainty, and at this altitude.

Nadir made what seemed to have been his first independent decision on route, and took himself, and his black stallion straight up the hill. We tried to follow. Very quickly it became clear that the hill was much steeper than expected. The route around the top, although passable, looked less promising than expected. It lead to a point well above the bottom of the glacier, with no obvious route down again. A pointless, fierce exchange between Nadir and me resulted in a stand-off between his stallion and two of the mares high on the hill. Tempers frayed. I had premonitions of being so near, and yet failing at the last moment. I jettisoned my horse, and started down the cliff side, telling Nadir and Sheffi to do the same, and to send the horses back with one of the three horsemen.

This expanse of glacial moraine was fearsome. There were boulders up to four or five metres high, piled up everywhere, and no obvious path through the jumble, to the glacier, and nothing to guide our decisions. Climbing over and around these smooth, slippery boulders became increasingly awkward. We were tired, irritable and in a hurry: a recipe for injury. Then we ran into two streams rushing between the boulders. They were strong, and cold, even for the Wakhis, but not impassable in width and depth; the problem was finding a place to cross. We contemplated trying to skirt the rivers and cross higher up, but decided against this, as we didn't know how far we would have to go. It was guesswork.

It took another half hour or more hour to deal with the problem, by creating man-bridges and swinging each other across, leaving the more agile Sheffi to last. The boulder clamber continued. Our precious time was draining away. I could see Anthony, now some hundred metres ahead; he had taken a better route. He was also fitter than me. Dillon was between us. We could not see the glacier; the view was blocked by hills of loose shale moraine, the size of double-decker buses and as secure as quicksand. It was hard to see how hills so high could have been created by the glacier unless its base had been moving backwards. The slate dunes absorbed feet and legs in plunging steps that advanced only inches a time. Sheffi had got ahead of all of us and was valiantly cresting the first of them, from where, I hoped to see a wave of success, an indication that he could see the glacier base. Instead he merely glanced and scrambled over the top, and then down, presumably to tackle the next one. I was fighting for air, and strength, and not for the first time conscious of a little extra weight around the middle, despite what I must have lost in recent days.

Anthony was ahead again, and higher, trying to reach the top of the same hill Sheffi had climbed. Then Sheffi reappeared; this time he was waving enthusiastically at us. Almost reluctantly I set off up the shale again. The view ahead had been reduced to two more remaining hills, but beyond that and below was churning water, indistinguishable in colour from its grey chalk shale channels, and beyond that was a black ice wall, and finally, a revelation….. There it was, at last, still some distance off, unexpectedly small, and dark, but surely this at last was the Ice Cave The entrance to the cave was not even a metre high. It was no more than a coal smile cracked into the mountainside. But flooding out from under the black ice of the low cave came a river.

We were still forty or so metres above. I was happy, but I had not actually managed to get down there to see into the cave. At that moment I could not face the extra effort of the climb there and back. It was a distance that at low altitude would have posed no problem, but here it was increasingly difficult and I was using most of my energy in just breathing.

Dillon, thank goodness, had other ideas, and set off without a word down the shale. Anthony followed, and after a deep breath or two, so did I. Only a few minutes later Dillon was down at the river edge and looking excitedly to his left. When I struggled to where he had reached, I could see why. It was then clear that the bulk of the water was not coming from the black cave, and indeed the black cave was not what we thought it was. Instead hitherto hidden behind the moraine was something much bigger, much more impressive, something almost frightening. Here was a white wall, sheer for twenty metres, then sloping off up the mountain. At its base there opened a hole, upturned cauldron shaped, may be ten or so metres wide and almost as high. And from it came not a stream or a trickle but a deep wide gush, flowing as if from the belly of the mountain itself. Here was indeed exactly what I had secretly sought all along. This was the Ice Cave, the open navel of the mountain, the way to its secrets. We were intruders in its private place that had remained mainly undisturbed for centuries.

Official source or not, this is how a river should be born; not at a little spring in Lechlade, like the Thames, or a quiet pool in the Rockies. This was a river born fully formed, belching and bellowing from the very heart of the Roof of the World. Its water was almost certainly was coming from ice formed beyond even the end of the Wakhan and in the Karakorum, where three countries and five great mountain chains meet in the very apex of the Pamir Knot.

There had clearly been a recent roof collapse, which had filled the base with ice fall, but there could be no doubt at all that this was the cave found by Curzon. In every way, the caves and surroundings met the description in Curzon's report to the Royal Geographical Society.

Nadir and Mirza Mohammed had not come down into the amphitheatre of the Ice Caves. It was a pity for them because they were also now enthused with their own interest in the river. But by the time we had scrambled and crawled back up the moraine towers to where they were watching from above, they had, following the tradition of the mountains, built a little memorial cairn out of stones to celebrate the journey.

When we got down again, through the boulder field, it became quickly clear that the horses were nowhere to be seen, and certainly had not been brought down into the valley where we were to exit. When we found them, it was getting dark, and progress became much more dependent on the skill of the animals in the fading light. I made the mistake of giving my warm clothing to Sheffi, who rode off far ahead, forgetting that he had it. For a long ride I was gradually freezing in semi summer wear, while I could see Sheffi, oblivious, in the far distance. It had been dark a long time when we finally reached camp. I must have had six successive cups of the ubiquitous tea before I was even ready to talk.

We were up early the next day to re-cross the rushing Diwanasu River before it became too strong. We marched on, retracing our steps back down the Wakhan Valley, but stopped early, around three thirty, and set up camp on a grassy bluff overlooking the river.

It was a very hot day, perhaps our hottest. But late in the afternoon a strong wind blew in, and it became cold again. Ahead of us, in the distance, was the cornflower sky that sheltered us most days; but behind us, from where we had come, it was a very different colour. It looked as if the devil had risen over the Pamir Knot and punched it in the eye. It was purple, chestnut and maroon, backlit with an orange fire, from the setting sun; the mountains it seemed were boiling a storm to chase us back from their secrets.

Shortly before dinner, a young Kirghiz boy, the only traveller we were to see in the Wakhan-i-Pamir, arrived in camp looking for a moment's respite. We gave him tea. He was only about fifteen years old, with an androgynous looking face, so that for a while I thought he was a girl, even though he was dressed in cast-off Russian military clothes, with a red headscarf. But no female would be out travelling alone and stopping to talk to a camp full of strangers. We tried to persuade him to stay the night with us, as it was now cold, and getting dark. But after drinking the tea, he mounted his donkey and departed. He was small, but the donkey was so tiny that the boy's feet were touching the ground as he rode off into the semi-darkness.

As night fell, the weather changed, and the rain started. We had not seen rain in Wakhan since a few drops in Ishkashem but this made up for two dry weeks. It was a storm with all the fireworks; the horses had sensed its coming long before we had, and they set up a whinnying chorus across the Pamir. There was little else we could do, but get into the shelter of our tents as the rain and wind increased in strength. I lay for a long time guiltily warm and dry, wondering how our team were faring with no

Above: Married Kirghiz women wear white headdresses
Below: Our distribution of sunwear has medical rather than fashion
utility at this altitude

Above: At the Ice Cave; the author, Antony Kitchin, Dillon Coleman
Below: One of the many Wajkir river contributaries

Above: Morning after the storm
Below: Kirghiz chieftain with his grandson during access negotiations

Above: Wakhan-i-Pamir and Little Pamir River
Below: Author with Chief of the Kirghiz nomads and the local leader
in the Little Pamir

Above: The Chelab stream
Below: Mirza catching trout by hand

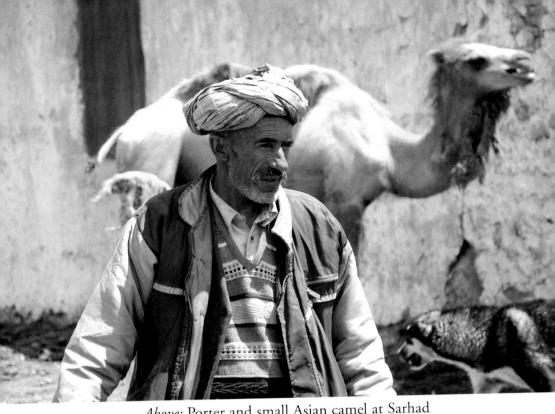

Above: Porter and small Asian camel at Sarhad
Below: Boys of the Wakhan

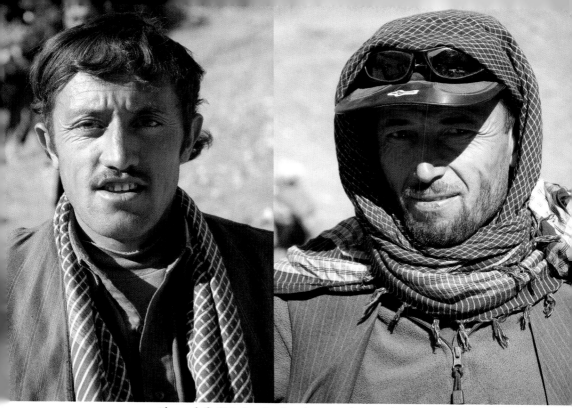

Above left: 'Holecdoc', *above right:* Nadir
Below left: Shafi, *below right:* Noseboy

Above: Author and the Sarhad Innkeeper
Below: An oasis on the Oxus north of Ishkashem

shelter other than their Russian blankets and a few rudimentary tarpaulins, more often used as table cloths.

As the noise of the rain decreased I relaxed and slept for several hours. When some light began to show, I unzipped my inner tent and then pulled at the outer zip. It came back and the canvas fell away, but it was strangely quiet, and I could see nothing. The rain in the night had turned to snow. The whole camp was covered in a deep, white duvet. The men were already awake; maybe they had not slept. I hardly dared enquire how they had fared through the night. But they astonished me with their equanimity. 'Just one of those things God sends us. We have seen worse. It is over and needs no further comment'. I had been impressed with the Afghans all through the journey, but never more so than that morning.

The reward for all of us was the astounding beauty of the newly white Pamir. I wondered all day, how the travelling boy had survived, and also from where he had come, since there were no more camps to the east. The Kirghiz camp where we had been given cooking lessons was now deserted, with just one solitary yurt left standing.

Mirza Mohammed and Nadir at the Ice cave in front of the
commemorative cairn that they built

CHAPTER SIXTEEN

رود خانه السوس

An Investigation in the Little Pamir with an interesting outcome

We had by now seen Syr Kul, the Ice Cave and the Little Pamir River. The one claimant that we had not seen was Lake Chakmaktin, favoured by Earl Dunmore and Colonel Trotter as the true source of the Oxus. So instead of returning over the Wakhan massif, we turned east up the Little Pamir in the usual sparkling, blue-brown, high altitude Wakhan morning.

But it was not only to see Lake Chakmaktin though; we had another mission, the one that had been at the back of my mind since the start of the journey. Was there another possible answer to the Oxus riddle that none of the 19th Century explorers had considered?

It was clear, and has been since the late 19th-century explorations, that Chakmaktin, which is very close to the Little Pamir watershed, empties to the east. It is a mirror image of Syr Kol in the Big Pamir and at a similar height, and not greatly different in size. These are the two parent lakes of the Oxus system. Chakmaktin itself is fed from a number of head rivers arising in the snow-belt above. These rivers by mid July would be quiet compared with, for example, a river primarily fed by glacier such as the

Wakhjir. Similar rivers feed the Little Pamir (or Scottish River as we had come to call it) which wandered down between our camp and the Wakhjir valley.

I wanted to explore the northern side of the Little Pamir, since I'd had an idea, which first occurred to me after studying some detailed Russian military maps, and I had enthused an initially sceptical Dillon with the prospect. Anthony stayed behind to bring into action, finally, the fishing rod that he had carried all the way from Sligo. We watched him, a lone, tiny figure picking his way down to the river, as we rode east along the Little Pamir.

We crossed several small streams and rode up the wide valley to a plateau, where I fully expected to find Lake Chakmaktin. I should by now have understood that any such expectation is never quite realised so simply, and it took many, many more crests in the rolling Pamir before we could see the sparkling bracelet of the lake.

We kept close to the north side of the Pamir for several hours. At one point two of the horsemen rode up into the hills to a Kirghiz settlement that was out of sight to us, apparently to get a supply of bread. It seemed like a very long diversion for a few wheels of bread, and I wondered, in this land of the poppy, whether there might be another attraction in the settlement. We marked off each successive small side valley on the map, and closed on the lake. Ahead and due east, Little Pamir stretched out to the end of Wakhan and the snow topped mountains that formed part of the Tajik–Afghan–Chinese border. These seem to have a much lower snow line than the immediate Pamir peaks, and formed a distant backdrop that reflected in the delphinium blue of Lake Chakmaktin, when it eventually emerged.

We were concentrating our attention on a side valley which the Wakhis called the Chelab and seemed to be the biggest feeder for Chakmaktin. The typical mountain river creates a V-shaped valley and continues until it meets and joins a similar river and so on until the combined flows exit the mountains, or reach the sea. It seemed possible that the Chelab followed a different course, falling from the mountain and then splitting into two.

The only way this could happen would be if the valley, or approach to the valley, into which it falls is on a flat plane.

One place where a Pamir is likely to be close to flat, is at a watershed within the range, i.e. at the highest point along the Pamir, where the natural direction of water flow changes. This unusual effect can be seen in both the Big and the Little Pamir, which run parallel to each other either side of the Afghan–Tajik border. In each case a point is reached along the Pamir where water that has been flowing gradually east, is pooled, and then a little further on, is flowing in the opposite direction. It is not surprising that at such points a lake would typically form, even in very flat land close to the watershed. We had seen exactly this phenomenon when searching for Syr Kul nearly two weeks earlier, and just eighty kilometres to the north and west of where we now were. The topography around Lake Chakmaktin and Syr Kul is almost identical in this respect.

My idea was that the Chelab valley might provide the source for both Chakmaktin and the Little Pamir River. It certainly provided the former. But could it possibly also have a division into two resulting in a branch flowing west, on the opposite watershed, to become the Little Pamir River?

If it were so, it would have remarkable implications for the arguments about the source of the mighty Oxus, as it might unify in the most unexpected way, two of the four claimed sources of the river. This would call into question many of the most important the calculations by Curzon and the others.

In effect two of the four contenders for 'Source of the Oxus', the Little Pamir river source and the Chakmaktin/Murghab sources, historically favoured by the explorers of the late 19th century until Curzon, would become one, and one with a serious claim to be the properly recognised source.

However it became increasingly likely that I was wrong, as we had clearly passed the watershed, and were following what seemed to be the river from the Chelab valley across the Pamir towards the lake. There were many dry watercourses, which would have been full a few weeks earlier. We followed likely ones but they all seemed to be running east. We consulted the horsemen who knew the Little Pamir; they all seemed to give a strong negative to our idea.

It was a glorious, soft and windless day. As we took our lunch near the lake we could have been on a grouse moor in August. Other than the disappointment of apparently dashed theories it was a memorable event for the fishing expedition that followed. We were now closer to the shore of the lake and the little river had divided into several smaller streams, one of which seemed to be rich with trout. Fish had not been part of our menu on this trip, and the thought of it was tempting.

Sheffi was watching the fish carefully. He stripped off the baggy trousers of his shalwar kameez and tied the bottoms together. Two of the Wakhi grabbed it from him and jumped into the clear waters, holding the open end wide in the current, shouting at the others to chase fish down river. Within a few minutes there were shrieks of excitement from the fishermen, and the pyjama was held high in the air, to show two captured trout. They caught six more this way. Then a new fisherman joined in. This was Mirza Mohammed, the one of the big hands and bright green hat, who had accompanied the Ice Cave party. He watched the others, then lay down beside the stream, put his hand into the water and appeared to be feeling around in the reeds. Moments later, with a shout and a huge grin, he leaped up, holding a wriggling trout. This was real sport. Within fifteen minutes he had taken another six or more fish out of the river, simply by searching them out under the reeds, where he expected them to hide, coming up behind and grabbing them with the massive Mirza paw.

I did not want to give up the search for the river flowing west without one more crossing back towards the Chelab valley, which was still directly to the north, so we headed west. Here, although from a distance, the Pamir looked flat, it was again a series of hidden undulations. Each time we came to a new crest I hoped to see a river flowing away from us, but all we found was a few dried or drying channels that could not reasonably be called in aid of the theory.

And then, almost when we had given up hope, there it was, over a small bank. From the moment we saw it there was no doubt whatsoever. It was a not just a meandering stream like the one we fished, but a forty to sixty foot deep valley cut by the river, now no more than a six foot stream. Our eyes followed the flow upstream, and it clearly flowed directly down the side valley from the Chelab source. There was no other possibility. The only way we could have missed the westward river on our trek earlier in the day was simply that we had crossed the Chelab above rather than below the division or bifurcation.

To be absolutely sure, we followed the new river downstream. It flowed west, and was indeed, the Little Pamir River itself, as eventually, apart from some peregrinations around obstacles, we followed it the whole way back to Bozai Gumbaz, where Anthony was probably still fishing, and the confluence with the Wakhjir.

So Lake Chakmaktin and the Little Pamir River, have the same source. Certainly the Chelab is not the only source for Lake Chakmaktin, but it was clearly the biggest and most significant. Without doubt, from our observations the Chelab is also the parent stream to the Little Pamir River; there is in fact no other substantial contributary until the Wakhjir confluence.

This is an inherently unlikely proposition as it depends on two coincidences, both running counter to every reasonable expectation. The first being that a single river, sourced in the Wakhan range between the Big and the Little Pamir, should divide into two or more streams right on the cusp of the Pamir mountain watershed; the second that the two resulting rivers should each create the respective sources of the eastwards (Lake Chakmaktin/Aksu/ Murghab) branch and westwards (Pamir River, Wakhan River) contributaries to the our great river.

But it seemed to be true. In effect, two adjacent molecules of water could descend the Chelab, as we called it, from the name of its valley, to the Little Pamir, then separate; one heading to Chakmaktin, and the other heading west towards Sarhad; and meet again later at Roshan Vomar, north of Khorog, 380 kilometres downstream in one direction and 360 in the other. We had found the Sorhab and Rustum of Afghan rivers, separated at birth, and joined later in life.

Wood, Dunmore, Trotter, Younghusband and Curzon had all in turn, stood over a piece of water, and with confidence, claimed to have found the true 'parent stream' of the Oxus. Some of them may have stood where we then stood, but without knowing what we knew. Even the confident Curzon would have had to acknowledge the facts, if he had realized that two of his competitor sources were actually one and the same. Dillon and I in our turn, stood looking down at an otherwise unimportant four foot width of water, and could follow, by eye, the course up towards its own source above us. We did not follow up the Chelab Valley. That valuable additional journey is still to be done; the first succeeding traveller will be able to claim the location of the source itself up the mountain to the north. (Marked O on the map on pages 8/9)

I knew there and then, that this was it. So many years of reading, and so much anticipation gave extra poignancy to the moment, whatever its lack of practical significance. This little stream really was what they had all sought for so long.

A few hours later we arrived back at 'Younghusband's camp' full of tales for Anthony and the rest of the team about what we had found. We were equally pleased about the fish, and how we caught them, only to find that Anthony had trumped us with the fly rod; his fish were already cooking on the fire. For the Irishman this was much more important than the minutiae of watersheds, bifurcations and river sources. He was right: crisp brown river trout, smelling sharp and smoky from the fire, crinkled baked potatoes and honeyed black tea, eaten again in front in front of that incomparable vista, the Halfway House to Heaven. That is what made me feel like the envy of all Asia.

POSTSCRIPT

Back across the river in Tajikistan we met Ergash again. It was not clear why but a change had come over him. Gone was the Toyota Landcruiser; gone was the skilled Hossein, whom we had planned to recruit into international motor rallying. Instead we had a very tired Russian jeep and a trainee driver. Ergash demoted himself to sitting in the luggage compartment. We ran out of gas within half an hour, and had to beg some off a passing vehicle, in fact the only passing vehicle we saw for most of the day. The new driver was on lesson one of his driving career; skills such as the use of gears, and the knowledge of which side of the road is customary for driving in Tajikistan had been deferred to lesson two.

But that was of no consequence because this was one of the world's most glorious riparine journeys. We were back with our river and its character was changing. Gone was its brash youthfulness in the Wakhan; now it was testing its adolescent strength and aggression in the gorges and switchbacks past Ishkashem and northwards through the western Pamirs to Khorog. Many times over it has to force its way through steep, narrow defiles, churning grey white against the rocks. The river is defining the country. It is a Moses of a river pushing regions apart. There is no running it on the northward swing; it is too wild. I never saw a boat or even a fisherman on the Oxus.

On the Tajik side the road, cut out of the mountain, runs alongside the river the whole way. On the Afghan side is a small donkey track that winds up and down the face, either on the bank by the river or sometimes forced high above via small ledges. Here is a marvellous potential journey that has probably never been done by Europeans: take the Afghan side path on foot with donkey all the way from Ishkashem to the bridge at Khorog or even beyond. It passes many villages, most of which will not have seen many outsiders and most likely will welcome guests.

Every few kilometres there are oases of life on one side or other... mellow greens and yellows of willows, poplars, with little patches of corn, vegetables, and fruit trees fed by irrigation channels running between the village houses. The colouring is softer here. There has been more erosion. There is reddish soil and vegetation waving in the summer winds, a scene reminiscent of the lowland valleys of Nepal.

Sometimes the villages are beside the river, sometimes higher up where springs or streams feed small cultivations. Afghan-Tajiks face Tajik-Tajiks across the river with apparently little communication between them.

Now towards Khorog, the Oxus is gaining maturity, becoming bolder and more assured in the big mountains. Beyond it spreads, swells and calms a little. The young ferocity under control, our river is growing up and searching for a mate. A hundred kilometres later a mate is what he finds. All the way from home back on the Little Pamir she comes. The other half of our little Chelab stream has turned east and flowed into Chakmaktin Lake, then out and down the Pamir before turning north into Tajikistan, past Murghab, through Lake Bartang, then due West to Vomar/Roshan.

The two small trickles from the Chelab valley have matured, faced all the adventures of separate 350-kilometre journeys, describing opposing circles through the Pamir, and met again here at Roshan. The two branches are married into the one mighty Oxus in its prime, the Oxus that had been our guide through its own country. Sorhab has found again his Rustum.

We left for Moscow, but
'The majestic river floated on…'.

Appendix I
Alexander Houghton Gardiner

Alexander Houghton Gardiner 1785-1877

If everything that Alexander Houghton Gardiner claims is true, then as John Keay (*Where Men and Mountains Meet*) writes "…the wanderings of Alexander Gardiner are perhaps the most remarkable in the whole field of nineteenth century travel in Asia. Single-handed and without any official support or geographical training, this man had, by 1831, already explored the Western Himalayas. Ten years before Vigne gave up his attempt to reach Gilgit, Gardiner had been there. Twenty years before Thomson tackled the Karakorum Pass, Gardiner had crossed it. Forty years before Shaw and Hayward reached Yarkand, Gardiner had passed through the city. And fifty years before an Englishman reached Kafiristan, Gardiner had returned there a second time. He had crossed every one of the six great mountain systems before maps even acknowledged their individual existence and he had seen more of the deserts of Turkestan than any non-Asiatic contemporary".

He was the one traveller that was to publicly claim that he had already reached the source of the Oxus before Lieutenant Wood. In fact he claimed to have found nineteen different sources, but he never provided any geographical detail to enable his contemporaries or others to identify even one of them. He wrote notes for flamboyant memoirs, but provided too little substantiation for his contemporaries to be able to properly judge his remarkable accounts and feats.

He was a cowboy, a soldier, a desperado, and a military Vicar of Bray. He fought for whomever paid him; he had no moral scruples of any sort about the methods to be used to secure his own safety, and his own ends. Lord Salisbury was to assert "the Englishman's right to get his throat cut wherever he wished"; he could have had Gardiner in mind, even though Gardiner did not admit to being English.

He maintained that he was born in Wisconsin, around 1785 and that his family migrated down the Mississippi to the area of New Orleans. He reached Asia via Ireland, and arrived at Kandahar in SE Afghanistan around 1830. If this was true, then the first Westerner of the modern era to search for, and maybe find the source of the river would have been an American, who had upstaged all the British, French and Russians of his time. The University of Wisconsin stills heralds Gardiner as their own Central Asian explorer, Wisconsin's very own contribution to the Great Game.

Gardiner was a wild looking and imposing man. Well over six foot, lean, strong, heavily bewhiskered, and often wearing a sword, and a full suit of the red tartan of the Lochiel Cameron. He was unable to swallow any food as a result of wound to the throat. He therefore carried a sort of iron collar, which he had to hold clamped to his neck in order to enable him to consume even liquids. He was a loner, and nonconformist. He was one of those who were only really happy when his ventures were not quite legal, or authorised, when the objectives were hidden, and the means questionable.

But to be recognised and approved it was not enough just to go, one had to report and convey to the public, and the geographers, realistic accounts of what you did and found. Gardiner had no maps, and made no effort to calibrate his journeyings beyond the vaguest references to time and distance. This was an age when there were any number of charlatans masquerading as genuine explorers, and often it took considerable detective work to tell the false from the true. Even the true were certainly given to embellishment, exaggeration and licence in their tales; the tales were hard to check, but the public wanted a little glamour to go with their geography.

The Royal Geographical Society (RGS) had effectively assumed the role of mother hen to travellers, and also the role of judge and referee in assessing their claims and stories. Frequently the *Journal* of the RGS would consist of almost as much questioning and criticism as new material. The two Sir Henrys, Yule and Rawlinson, were amongst the leading commentators. Yule, an ex-Indian Army Colonel was one of the most respected commentators on Central Asia, and received the Gold Medal of the RGS. Rawlinson was renowned as the decipherer of cuneiform, and was President of the RGS in the 1870s. Their joint scholarship in language, history, geography, and Asiatic nomenclature wholly qualified them for the task. Yule was to say of Gardiner's first rather sketchy diaries: "Geography, like divinity has its Apocrypha….I am sorry to have include under this head the diary of Colonel Gardiner". Rawlinson was just as scathing; "the diary reads more like a romance than a journal of actual adventure".

But Yule, Rawlinson and others were desk-bound scholars, whereas Gardiner started with no information and no learning. He was not their sort of traveller. He travelled where maps did not exist. He knew nothing of the RGS, or their academic needs. He had already broken new ground on many routes, probably without even knowing it. But he was clearly a story teller; all the firsthand accounts of him, particularly later in his life confirmed that this was his main occupation.

Some of the stories told by, or about, Gardiner have indeed been corroborated, but not those of his early life in the US, his participation in the War of Independence, his time in Ireland, or how he got to Central Asia in the first place, which according to him was via Egypt and Persia, and included lessons in gunnery, as well as time in the British Army.

Things become clearer following his arrival in Afghanistan, where he took up as a soldier of fortune and hired gun. He killed three of the local warlord's men near Kunduz to escape capture. He was attached again in Kohistan, but this time there were fifty or more opponents, the henchmen of Habibullah Khan, the enemy of Dost Mohammed, the then Afghan monarch in Kabul. He was captured but avoided death by offering to become a local commander under Habibullah Khan, and started to use the name Gurdana Khan.

During a raid to try to capture a princess from the harem of Dost Mohammed, he wrote that he saw the face of a beautiful young girl, and rode beside her. When his mercenary employer offered to share the spoils of the raid, Gardiner asked only to be allowed to take the girl as his wife.

They lived together for a two years and a son was born. He enjoyed some domestic tranquillity but it was soon cruelly destroyed. Khan's forces had been heavily defeated by Dost Mohammed. Gardiner escaped and succeeded in returning home to find that his own fort had been attacked.

"The silence was oppressive when I rode through the gateway of the fort, and my men instinctively fell back, when an old mullah, who had remained faithful to our party, came out to meet me with his hands bound. His fingers had been cut off and his arm nearly severed by scimitar blows whilst he was trying to protect my child. Faint from his wounds and from the miserable recollection of the scene he at first stood gazing at me in a sort of wild abstraction, and then recounted the tale of the massacre of all that I loved.

He beckoned to me silently to follow him into the inner room. There lay four mangled corpses – my wife, my boy, and two little eunuchs. I had left them thoughtless and happy but five days before. The right hand of the hapless young mother could be seen, and clenched in it, the reeking katar with which she had stabbed herself to the heart after handing over the child to the priest for protection. Her room had been broken into, and mortally wounded as she was, the assassins had nearly severed her head from her body with their long Afghan sabres. The mullah had tried to escape with the child, but had been cut across the hand and arm, the boy seized and barbarously murdered. There he lay by the side of his mother.

I sank on my knees and offered a prayer for vengeance to the most high God. Tear after tear trickled down the pallid cheeks of the priest as he uttered the Mohammedan prayers for the dead. Rising, I forced myself away from the room, gave all the money I had for the interment of the dead, and with fevered brain rode away for ever from my once happy mountain home."

(from Memoirs of Alexander Gardiner, Col H Pearse as quoted in the notes to George Macdonald Fraser's *Flashman and the Mountain of Light*)

So tragically free of ties in Afghanistan, he renounced for a while his mercenary life, and set off to explore the Western Himalayas.

His journal then becomes very confused and indistinct. It is clear that eventually he reached Chinese Turkestan and Yarkand. His reports of the area are reasonably plausible but the journey starts in 1826 and the next date given is nearly four years later. The intervening wanderings provide virtually no useful information about his route, or his means of travel. None of the obvious land marks are mentioned after the initial intention to cross the Oxus, at what would seem to be Ishkashem, where the river emerges from the Wakhan and begins its long sweep north through the Eastern Pamirs of what is now Tajikistan. He describes finding and following nineteen different 'sources' of the river but does not provide geographical details to enable them to be checked against the maps of the time or later.

Thereafter his tale becomes more plausible and verifiable. He was appointed an Officer in the army of Ranjit Singh in Lahore, in what is now the north of Pakistan. Ranjit Singh was the feared, but admired Maharajah of the Punjab. He had succeeded his father at the age of twelve and managed to unite the Punjab under his sole command. He ruled Punjab as the only northern state not controlled by the British. Justifying again his reputation of somehow managing to come out on the winners' side, Gardiner was one of the very few who survived the wild, barbaric dark days that followed Ranjit's death. Almost all those struggling to take over his or parts of his Empire were murdered or somehow eliminated. It is highly likely that Gardiner actually took on the role of enforcer for one of them. He is thought to be the man who personally cut off the thumb, nose and ears off Brahmin Jodha Ram. John Keay writes : "There is no question that Gardiner did wield the razor….but in those turbulent times few survived with their lives, let alone their dignity intact; there were certainly extenuating circumstances".

One survivor of the internecine conflict, supported by the British, was Ghulab Singh, whose character Gardiner described as "one of the most repulsive it is possible to imagine". However not long after he was to take up employment with the same Ghulab Singh, then created Maharajah of Kashmir. He became commandant of the new Maharajah's artillery and remained as such until his retirement into reminiscence, conviviality, and the company of girlfriends, whom he continued to charm.

Gardiner lived in Kashmir until his death at the age of 92 in 1877. He died peacefully in bed, an end which must have seemed most unlikely throughout the previous forty years, though his dead body is reported to have shown evidence of at least fourteen serious injuries

Contemporary views of Gardiner were as divided as those of later commentators. He was to earn the recognition, and even admiration of many of the most lauded Central Asia men of the later 19th century, such as Shaw Hayward, Godwin-Austen and Ney Elias. The latter argued that his intimacy with so many of the places he claimed to have visited could not have been absorbed from others. However he was excoriated as an impostor, a liar and a brute in a carefully reasoned review by C. Grey, the author in 1929 of the encyclopaedic *European Adventurers of Northern India*.

Gardiner probably was in part both a successful adventurer and fantacist. He could hardly have survived the many changes of fortune and circumstance, particularly in Afghanistan and Lahore from 1830 to 1845 without taking on roles, and using subterfuge. He was a master of storytelling, in all its guises, and used this to his advantage, but he did not invent all of his travelling tales. Indeed if they were all invented or borrowed from others that he met in Lahore, as Grey suggests, where was he in those lost years? However the record of his early life, his American/Irish background, and the jouneyings to Central Asia lack substance. It is much more likely that he was another deserter from the British India forces, either naval or army. He was so clearly a maverick and an individualist; one cannot imagine him remaining long in the ranks, and he would have known that preferment as an officer was virtually impossible. How much more satisfactory to desert, reappear in Afghanistan with an invented past and some useful military learning, where he could take up a much more senior role? Fifteen or twenty years later his invented past was already too well established to discard, and anyway, desertion was a very serious crime, punishable without any statute of limitations. The web was woven and it must have been much easier to live within its ambit.

Appendix II
Ney Elias

Ney Elias 1844-1897

The authority to whom Curzon turned for authentification of his conclusions about the geography of the upper Oxus was Ney Elias. He alone amongst Europeans had seen the confluence of the two branches of the Oxus. For explorers of Curzon's generation, Ney Elias was the father figure of Central Asian Exploration.

Extract (written by the author) from The Great Explorers, *Thames and Hudson 2010, Editor Robin Hanbury Tenison*

In 1873 two men were chosen to stand in front of the gathered Fellows of the Royal Geographical Society to receive its highest accolade, the Founders' Medal. The two were recognised as the greatest explorers of their time and were equally illustrious both within the Society and amongst the general public for their achievements. One, Henry Morton Stanley, remains a recognised hero in the history of exploration; the other, Ney Elias, is almost completely forgotten. Stanley's good fortune was that he travelled in Central and Southern Africa, where British colonial interests would be focussed for the next century; he was subsequently to be seen as a pioneer of a whole period of British history. Elias however travelled in China and Central Asia, far more important politically and economically in the mid-19th-century world than Africa, but later to be comparatively disregarded whilst Britain and Europe spent much of the next century pursuing local conflicts and Central Asia was to become mainly closed to foreigners. A different course of history would have seen Stanley, Burton, Speke, Mungo Park and others forgotten, whilst later generations celebrated Younghusband, Przhevalsky, Bonvalot and most of all, Ney Elias.

But there is another reason for his relative obscurity today; he did almost nothing to court fame as an explorer. The more typical Asian travellers, like 'Bokhara' Burnes, would seek trophy destinations and then speed back to London to trumpet their achievements. Elias eschewed personal publicity. The public knew almost nothing about him, particularly his private life. He was one of those many 19th-century and later travellers, who travelled partly because they felt safer away from social expectations. He had no known relationships with women. He had this in common with his Russian contemporary, Nicolai Przhevalsky. They also had in common an apparently fearless determination to proceed whatever the odds against them. Each was their country's outstanding Central Asian explorer.

Elias was born in 1844 into a Jewish merchant family in Bristol and was sent to school in Dresden, where he was alone away from his family for two years. He was expected to join the family firm, and this took him to their office in Shanghai. It was quickly clear that Ney's bent was for discovery rather than commerce.

He started in 1868, exploring in three journeys, the remarkable Yellow River, which had just gone through one of its periodic gyrations and altered course to flow north east instead of south east and emerge into a different sea altogether. But Elias's mind was already elsewhere and his ambition was to reach 'the civilisation surrounded by deserts' or Chinese Turkestan and Kashgaria, the Moslem-dominated areas in the shadow of the Tien Shan mountains at the far western end of China.

The second expedition, the one that undoubtedly made his name, was a Herculean journey. He left Peking in July 1872, travelling alone, picking up guides as best he could along the way. He went north to Mongolia, across the Gobi, north of the Western deserts, ran into local fighting between loyal Chinese and Tartar Moslem rebels and eventually crossed the Russian border over the Altai Mountains. This was 2,700 miles at no better than about 15-20 miles a day, mainly walking, sometimes on horse or camel-back; and still he was only half way to his final destination, the start of the trans-Russia railway at Nijni Novgorod (Gorki) at the other end of endlessly cold and forbidding Siberia, which he crossed in what was by then mid-winter. All the way he continued to take his observations and positional readings, which were eventually delivered to Kew Observatory.

Sir Henry Rawlinson, President of the RGS, described this second of Ney Elias's expeditions as "one of the most extraordinary feats of modern times, that would live in the memory long after other (journeys) are forgotten".

By then Elias had either run out of money or exhausted the patience of his family and needed income. He was quickly appointed as Extra Attaché of the Foreign Department of the Government of India and this began the major phase of his career as in effect a Government agent or spy. He was to hold a number of appointments but all disguised his real function, that of intelligence gatherer. For the next 15 years Elias would undertake another six major and many minor expeditions, often ostensibly as a private citizen but always in fact pursuing the interests of the British Empire in Asia. The expeditions were sometimes his initiative but more often the Viceroy or Foreign Office needed information about what the Russians and the Chinese were doing in Central Asia. The alternatives were either to send a fully equipped and publicly appointed mission or to waive formalities and leave it to Elias. Britain's greatest fear was the possibility of Russian designs on India, as their own Empire expanded so fast to the South. The standoff between the two Empires became known as the Great Game, a phoney war that was fought by gentleman explorers on both sides with hardly a shot being fired. Elias was the archetype and most experienced of all Britain's Great Gamers.

His first two missions were into Chinese Turkestan finding his way north from Hunza and Gilgit (now North Pakistan) across the forbidding Karakorum Mountains to Kashgar, which then as now was the centre of power, information and politics in Central Asia, a Turkic Uigur city but home to peoples of almost every ethnic group in Asia. It had recently been re-occupied by the Chinese.

The next was the Pamir or Roof of the World expedition, where he sought to discover the source of the Oxus in the Pamir Mountains. Crossing into Afghanistan from Chitral he became just the first Briton to explore the Pamir north of Lake Syr Kul (which Lt Wood had discovered in 1838). He claimed Rang Kul as the legendary Dragon Lake of the Chinese Bhuddist pilgrims and spent months investigating and mapping the Pamirs, and was able to report back on the considerable difficulties that any potentially invading force would encounter.

There was an aura of impenetrability and mystery about the Pamir. So the Pamir journey further enhanced Ney's reputation as a fearless clandestine adventurer, particularly as once again he was alone and also by now struck with illness, probably amoebic dysentery.

He returned ill from the Pamirs but was soon recruited, as by far the most experienced China and Tibet watcher in the Indian Government, to go to Sikkim to help the Indian Government negotiate with Tibet/China in a political dispute that had overflowed into the little independent state of Sikkim. His final major expedition took him back to Burma to try to create recognised borders with Siam.

Even the other great names of Central Asian exploration looked up to Elias, partly because of his indisputable breadth of knowledge and experience and party because of his own refusal ever to be competitive about his career and achievements.

"Few of the Queens' servants in Asia have done so much and talked so little of what they have done". (Obituary notice for Ney Elias, *Times of India* 1897)

Appendix III
Greg Mortensen and the Central Asia Institute

Greg Mortensen's Stones into Schools

The north east of Afghanistan has been a battleground since 1979 and has suffered as much as any other part of the country. During the Soviet occupation it was a breeding ground for the Mujahadeen insurgency and not long afterwards the same guerrilla groups were fighting the Taliban. The independence campaign was born out of a confidence that the leaders knew what was right for their Badakshan province. It had been emaciated and impoverished, a region gasping for air by 2003, when Sadhar Khan, *Commandhan* in Baharak, first met the American, Greg Mortensen.

He greeted him with excited hugs. This was the 'Doctor Greg' he had long awaited. Mortensen was already a hero in the Northern Areas of Pakistan and the stories of his work has been brought across the borders.

Mortensen's humanitarian adventure that had excited the interest of Sadhar Kahn and established the reputation of his Central Asia Institute had started when Mortensen had attempted the ascent of K2 in 1993. He did not make it and was lost alone on his descent when he was rescued by the people of Korphe, one of the highest villages on earth. He spent several weeks there and when he left he promised to come back some day and build for them, and particularly for their entirely uneducated girls, a school. He was penniless but managed in the next three years to raise the money to do so. He returned money in hand to find that before the school was built, they really needed a bridge for communication with the rest of the country. He built both bridge and school and went on to build more than a hundred schools in the most northern areas of Pakistan and then Afghanistan. By 2009 there were more than sixty thousand children, mainly girls, in his schools. They had been built by the villagers for themselves out of whatever materials were available, funded, encouraged and planned by Greg's team. The inspiring story of his campaign to 'promote peace with books and not bombs' is told in his books *Three Cups of Tea* and *Stones into Schools*. He had built a team from people of all different religious and social groups. They had been drawn to his drive to achieve. Together they had faced and overcome prejudice against female education and had steadily earned the respect of those with influence and power for good in North Pakistan. Greg had been tried by one of the highest Islamic courts for supposed crimes against Islamic law. He was not only acquitted but the judgement issued and passed around the region confirmed that his work was in the direct interests of Islam and should be supported in every way possible. The consideration of the case and the judgement was for the West uncomfortably contemporaneous with the continued detention without trial or proper representation of the hundreds of inmates of the Guantanamo Bay detention camps.

Sahdar Khan and Mortensen had an immediate bond. Khan, himself one of the most celebrated of the Mujahadeen commanders, wanted a school for his village. He took Greg out to see the surrounding rocky hills.

"There has been far too much dying in these hills." he said. "Every rock, every boulder that you see before you is one of my Mujahadeen martyrs who has sacrificed his life fighting the Russians and the Taliban. Now we must make their sacrifice worthwhile. We must turn these stones into schools".

The first CAI school in Afghanistan was built in Baharak and there followed schools building programmes throughout the region and even into Wakhan. The programme developed to include career clubs, adult learning centres and reading clubs for Afghan women.

One great ambition remained to be achieved for Greg. Back in 1999, Greg had been attending to the building of a school in the Charpurson valley close to Hunza in the Northern Areas of Pakistan. A delegation of horsemen came across the Irshad Pass. They were the same or representatives of the same Kirghiz nomads who had supported us in the Wakhan. They had heard of the schools building programme and came with the seemingly extraordinary suggestion that Greg should try to get to the High Pamir and build a school there, where no other buildings existed. Greg and his colleague, Sarfraz Khan, himself from the Charpurson valley, gradually became enthused by this outlandish idea. It represented the very pinnacle of their possible achievements and fitted exactly their idea that they should tackle first the most difficult and seemingly unapproachable regions for their humanitarian work. Greg referred to the Wakhan as the 'first last place', far the most difficult, far the most unlikely and therefore the most important school that he would ever try to build. As solemnly as he had six years before in Korphe he looked the leader of the horsemen in the eye and said; "Yes, I promise to come to build you a school".

The book *Stones into Schools* is the story of where that promise led Mortensen, his CAI and the team that had been created around them. It also tells the story of the growing influence that this most unlikely of military counsellors unexpectedly had over the course of the Afghan conflict. So much so that by 2009 Mortensen's advice is closely heeded by the US General Staff and his first book *Three Cups of Tea* is required reading for all US Special Forces.

A. A choice of the most enduring and exciting Central Asian literature and travel books...the real classics (some of these have to be obtained via second hand book sources):

Francis Younghusband: *Heart of a Continent* (the story of his epic trans-China journey and the 'epiphany' in the Karakorum). Although originally published in 1886 by John Murray (the 'father' publishing house for Central Asia travel), the best current edition is the 1984 Oxford University Press (Hong Kong) edition with Younghusband's marvellous contemporary map, still possibly the finest Karakorum/Pamir map ever printed.

Robert Byron: *Road to Oxiana* (Macmillan Co, London 1937 and many later editions).

Sir Fitzroy McLean: *Eastern Approaches*. (Johnathan Cape 1949) The diplomat's classic post-war adventures in the southern states of the Soviet Union

George Nathaniel Curzon: *The Pamirs and the Roof of the World*, (originally published in the Geographical Journal of the RGS 1895; republished 2005 by Elibron Classics)

Peter Fleming: *News From Tartary* (Johnathan Cape 1936) The story of his 1935 crossing of China and the Western deserts in particular. The same story is told as well by his companion Ella Maillart in her *Forbidden Journey* (Walter Heinemann 1937) Both do their best to disguise the fact they travelled together.

Peter Hopkirk: *Foreign Devils on the Silk Road* (John Murray 1980) and *The Great Game*. (John Murray 1990). Peter Hopkirk and John Keay *Explorers of the Western Himalayas* (John Murray 1996) are fine story tellers and the outstanding authorities on the Central Asia travel and exploration.

Greg Mortensen and David Relin: *Three Cups of Tea* (Viking Penguin 2006) See Appendix III

Galen Rowell: *Mountains of the Middle Kingdom* (Sierra Book Club 1983). The admired landscape photographer's essay and photo book about China and Central Asia's great mountains, together with the mountaineering history.

Eric Newby: *A Short Walk in the Hindu Kush* (1958 Secker and Warburg and many later editions).

Matthew Arnold's epic poem, *Sohrab and Rustum* (1853)

Mountstuart Elphinstone: *An Account of the Kingdom of Caubul* (1815; republished with the original maps by Munishiram Manoharial Publishers, New Delhi 1998)

B. Contemporary reports from 19th-century and other travellers

The Travels of Marco Polo (Liveright Publishing, New York 1926 from the 14th century original)

Sir Alexander Burnes: *Travels into Bokhara* (1834)

John Wood: 'Report of a Journey to the Sources of the Amu Darya', *Journal of the Royal Geographical Society* (1840), Vol 10

John Wood: *Journey to the Source of the Oxus* (Elibron Classics edition of John Murray 1872 revised edition with introduction by Wood's son, Alexander)

Robert Shaw: *Visits to High Tartary; Kashgar and Yarkand* (John Murray

1871 or Oxford University Press, Hong Kong 1984). Shaw was Younghusband's uncle and travel hero

Lt Col TE Gordon RE: 'The Watershed of Central Asia, East and West', *Geographical Journal of the RGS, (*1876), p.381

St George Littledale: 'A Journey across the Pamir from North to South' *Proceedings of the Royal Geographical Society,* 23 November 1891

Sir Francis Younghusband: 'Journeys in the Pamirs and Adjacent Countries', *Proceedings of the Royal Geographical Society*, 8 February 1892

Charles Adolphus Murray, Earl of Dunmore: 'Journeyings in the Pamir and Central Asia', *The Geographical Journal*, no. 5, Vol II, November 1893.

Charles Adolphus Murray, Earl of Dunmore: *The Pamirs*, Vols I and II, (originally published by John Murray 1893)

Captain H Bower: 'A Trip to Turkestan', *Proceedings of the Royal Geographical Society*, no. III, March 1895

George Nathaniel Curzon (later Viscount Kedleston and Viceroy of India): 'The Pamirs and the Source of the Oxus', *The Geographical Journals of the RGS*, July, August and September 1896; the *Proceedings* that record Curzon's famous lectures given over three successive meetings of the Royal Geographical Society. The final lecture is also distinguished by the recorded oral exchanges between Curzon, Younghusband, Colonel Trotter (on behalf of himself and Earl Dunmore), Gen Sir Thomas Gordon, Field Marshal Lord Roberts and the President of the RGS, Sir Clements Markham. A similar discussion is recorded between Younghusband, Sir Aurel Stein, Sir Henry Trotter and others in the *Geographical Journal* Vol. LXVIII, No.3, September 1916, which shows the Oxus River source question to be as alive and unsettled a question as it had been in 1895.

Captain H H P Deasy: 'Journeys in Central Asia' *The Geographical Journal of the RGS*, no.2, Vol XVI, August 1990 and no.5, Vol XVI, November 1990

'Report of the Proceedings of the Boundary Commission and subsequent dissenting correspondence by Lord Curzon (from Calcutta March 1899) and Lt Col Trotter (from Galatz, Rumania February 20 1899)', *The Geographical Journal of the RGS* (1899), Vol. XIII

Sir Aurel Stein : *Ancient Khotan* (1907)

Eric Shipton: *The Six Mountain Travel Books* (Diadem Books The Mountaineers, Seattle 1985)

Jean Bowie Shor: *The Trail of Marco Polo* (Shakespeare Head Press, London 1956 and later Travel Book Club edition).

C. Histories, stories and commentary

Sir Henry Rawlinson: *Monograph on the Oxus, Geographical Journal of the RGS,* (1872), Vol. XLII. This seminal Oxus article reviewed the history of Oxus myth and exploration. Rawlinson was President of the RGS 1874-5 and was also renowned as the decipherer of cuneiform.

Stephen Wheeler: 'Obituary of Ney Elias', *The Geographical Journal of the RGS,* 1897.

C Grey: *European Adventurers in Northern India 1785-1949* (Naval and Military Press)

Gustav Krist: *Prisoner in the Forbidden Land* and *Alone Through the Forbidden Land.* Extraordinary and at times barely believable stories of an escaped Austrian First World War prisoner in Turkic Central Asia (Readers Union edition 1939)

George Macdonald Fraser; *Flashman and the Mountain of Light* (Harvill Press 1990)and *Flashman in the Great Game* (Barrie and Jenkins 1975) The novels have detailed historical notes attached.

Donald Rayfield: *The Dream of Lhasa; Life of Nikolay Przhevalsky.* This short volume is the only English language book about the Russian explorer Przhevalsky, possibly the most distinguished of all the 19th-century travellers. (Elek Books, London 1976)

Dervla Murphy: *Where the Indus is Young* (Century Travellers edition 1983 of John Murray 1977 publication)

Peter Hopkirk: *On Secret Service East of Constantinople.* German, British and Russian secret services in Central Asia during the First World War;

sequel to the Great Game (John Murray 1994)

Peter Hopkirk: *Foreign Devils on the Silk Road* (Oxford University Press 1980)

Kathleen Hopkirk: *Central Asia, a Travellers Companion*, with a much more detailed bibliography than this one. (John Murray 1993)

Patrick French: *Younghusband*. The book that created a genre in which personal travel is entwined with biographical history (Harper Collins 1994)

Anke Seirstad: *The Bookseller of Kabul* (Little Brown 2003)

Khaled Hosseini: *The Kite Runner* (Bloomsbury 2003)

Elizabeth and Nicholas Clinch: *Land of Extremes, The Littledales of Central Asia* (The History Press 2008)

Greg Mortensen: *Stones into Schools*. (Penguin 2009) The second chapter of his epic campaign to build schools and learning in North Pakistan, Afghanistan and the Wakhan.

Gerald Morgan: *Ney Elias* (George Allen and Unwin 1971)

David Gilmour: *Curzon* This is the definitive political history. (John Murray 1994)

Hugh Leach; *A Ride to Shiwa, A Source of the Oxus* (Journal of the Royal Society of Asian Affairs Asiatic 1986 17:3). Hugh Leach's report of his discovery that the waters of Lake Shiwa (Kowl-e-Shiveh), Badakshan, discharge into the Oxus close to Khorog via subterranean flow and therefore that Shiwa itself is a source of the river.

C. Guide Books

Bijan Omrani and Matthew Leeming: *Afghanistan, Companion Guide* (Odyssey 2007)

Robert Middleton and Huw Thomas: *Tajikistan and the High Pamirs* (Odyssey 2008)

Laurence Mitchell;: *Kyrgyzstan* (Bradt Guides)

Giles Whittell: *Central Asia* (Cadogan Guides)

THANKS

I want to thank, in particular for their their good humour, friendship and and resourcefulness and for putting up with me, my companions Dillon Coleman and Antony Kitchin. All the photographs in this book are their work and copyright (none of my inadequate efforts survived the editorial pencil). Dillon's attention to geographical detail and records of names and places have also been a great help to me; his own upcoming book on the Oxus will no doubt soon eclipse this volume.

The journey that is described here was made possible only by the organization, support and comradeshipfriendship given by our Tajik, Afghan, Kirghiz and Wakhi colleagues: Ergash Fayzullobekov, our guide in Tajikistan and his skilled driver Hosein from Khorog; Afghans Mohammed Nadir, from Khosh, Mohammed Shafi from Darwaz, Badakshan and Ghulam Sahki Danishjo from the Shakh Ali district of Parwan Province, our team leaders in the Wakhan. The porters, cooks, horsemen, entertainers, adventurers, who too were our inspiration and whose generally happy dispositions and generous spirits are a reflexion of their glorious country: Mirza Mohammed and Menber; Wakhis Niaz Bai (Noseboy), Hamidullah and Shahpoor from Chelkan; Musafer, Murad, Shanbe, Sayed Qassem from

Ptukh; Satar from Neshtkhawr; Saifal, Khaleq Dad (Holecdoc), and Jama from Sarhad; Mehraban from Shelk and Afghan Burhanuddin from the Panjshir. Also it might not have happened without the help of the Great Game Travel people in Badakshan and Kabul.

The Aga Khan Foundation (Tom Kessinger, Director in Geneva and the small team in Ishkashem) did whatall they could to help us. AKF is almost alone in providing humanitarian aid and project development support in the Wakhan.

I learned much from Changez Sultan and PTDC in Islamabad and from histheir enthusiasm for and promotion of the beauty of North Pakistan and the Karakorum region during the early journeys. (Thanks for lending Inki and me your vehicle in 1988, Changez; you must have wondered if you would get it back intact or at all…and thanks from me and her family for your beautiful poem at her funeral).

For advice and help in advance I am indebted to:

Matthew Leeming (travel@matthewleeming.com) and Bijan Omrani, Central Asia historian, who also together wrote the *Odyssey Companion Guide to Afghanistan.*

Robert Middleton and his website (www.pamirs.com), who also introduced me to Ergash Fayzullobekov.

Julien Dufour and his website (www.juldu.com), a comprehensive source of information about Pamirs and the Wakhan.

My friends Georgie Cecil and Mouse Campbell, who had pioneered much of the route with more derring-do than ours, and crossed the Boroghil into Pakistan a few years before.

John Mock and Kimberley O'Neil (www.mockandoneil.com), guide book writers and experts on Wakhan, Pamirs, and the Karakorum., whose experience and adventures there far exceed my own.

Thanks also to Mr. Samir from the Tajik Embassy in Brussels, who untied the Gordian Knot of double entry visas for Tajikistan.

Also to Sir Ranulph Fiennes, Robin Hanbury Tenison and Geordie Torr, the editor of The Geographical Magazine for their encouragement; to Lieutenant General Simon Mayall, who over a long lunch at the Garrick

Club, or maybe in Provence, introduced me to stories about that wild man of the Pamir, Alexander Gardiner.

The Library team at the Royal Geographical Society were as helpful as always, as was Shane Winser, head of the Expeditions team.

This book simply would not have made its way into print without my editors, both very much more distinguished writers than I could ever hope to be. Anna Swan (*Statues Without Shadows* 2006) instructed me about structure, style and kindly alerted me to basic essentials that I would have missed. Neil Rollinson is a celebrated poet (*Spillage of Mercury*, *Spanish Fly* and others; www.neilrollinson.com). He has always been unjustifiably enthusiastic and encouraging, the sort of tutor everyone should have. He won the National Poetry Prize in 1997 and was a Judge for the same competition in 2009 and 2010. He has also been entertaining company for me and my publisher, Anthony Weldon, the eminence grise of Bene-Factum Books, the other sine qua non of Halfway House to Heaven. Map maker John Gilkes has enabled me to put some geographical sense into the narrative.

Thank you, Christian Larsson for your friendship, especially when most valued.

My apologies to my family, especially Soraya and Kara, who bore the brunt. I now know that 'I have to work on my book' is always a poor excuse to avoid doing something more pressing.

Thanks for the promptings of the tenth Muse, whose domain must be restlessness and adventure...